TO THE WALTROP FAMILY !

F. THORNE

02/17/08

The evacuated Elizabethtown patriots watch
helplessly as Reverend Caldwell's home is
torched by the retreating British forces.

FOR SENATOR
BOB CRANE

THE
ILLUSTRATED
HISTORY
OF UNION COUNTY

TEXT AND DRAWINGS
BY FRANK THORNE

FANTAGRAPHICS BOOKS

7563 Lake City Way
Seattle, WA 98115

Written and Illustrated by **Frank Thorne**
Production by **Paul Baresh**
Published by **Gary Groth and Kim Thompson**

Visit our website at **www.fantagraphics.com**

You may obtain a lovely,
full-color catalogue of comics absolutely free by calling toll-free

1-800-657-1100

ISBN: 1-56097-721-3

Printed in Canada.

Office Of The Mayor

CITY OF ELIZABETH, NEW JERSEY

J. CHRISTIAN BOLLWAGE
Mayor

CITY HALL
50 WINFIELD SCOTT PLAZA
ELIZABETH, NEW JERSEY 07201-2462

TEL. 908-820-4170
FAX 908-820-0130

FORWARD

The City of Elizabeth, called "Elizabethtown" in the 17th and 18th Centuries, was the original capitol of the great State of New Jersey. The first State Legislature convened here, as did the First State Supreme Court. Many of the legendary patriots, including George Washington, Alexander Hamilton and Aaron Burr were visitors to Elizabethtown.

The present City of Elizabeth is the fourth largest municipality in the State of New Jersey, and extends 11.7 square miles. As the Union County seat, Elizabeth is centrally located to the entire tri-state area and is home to the Jersey Gardens Mall, IKEA, and numerous small businesses. Elizabeth is a diverse cultural and transportation hub that continues to play a major role in the social, political, and economic activities of New Jersey and far beyond its borders.

I wish Frank Thorne, the creator of the series, and Dr. Neil Rosenstein, who re-discovered the newspaper feature of the early 1950's, much success with this publication and all of their future endeavors.

Sincerely,

Chris Bollwage
Mayor

INTRODUCTION

Arriving from South Africa in 1973 I settled in Union County and took up residence in Elizabeth. It was in the Union County Courthouse that I became a United States citizen. From 1975 until the present I have been a member of the medical and surgical staff of Trinitas Hospital in Elizabeth. I am also an avid researcher into various areas of history and genealogy.

Recently I was on the quest for information on David Naar, Elizabeth's only Jewish mayor, who served between 1842 and 1845. I made an extraordinary discovery while researching at the Elizabeth Public Library; specifically the microfilm files of the now defunct *Elizabeth Daily Journal,* which in the 1800's was a weekly called *The Jersey Journal.*

Browsing through the 1950 file I happened upon page after page of a unique daily feature titled *The Illustrated History of Union County* by Frank Thorne. The series, 173 strips in all, covered the county from the pioneer days through the settlement and industrialization in a vivid illustrative style. I felt that the series should be published so it might educate and entertain the current generation. A Google computer search quickly located the current whereabouts of Frank Thorne, creator of the series, then a lad of nineteen. Further Googling revealed Frank's incredible career; his many creations; among them *Red Sonja* for Marvel Comics that became a major motion picture starring Arnold Schwarzenegger; and his recently published novels.

I contacted Frank and found him receptive to my proposal that his history be gathered in book form. Being a published author myself I felt comfortable with our growing relationship. To our dismay none of the original artwork survived, so Frank had to resurrect the series by working with the yellowed newsprint images. He manually cleaned them up and replaced the crude hand lettering with a computer font. We worked together making the original text politically correct for today's climate.

I am now most delighted that the complete version of *The Illustrated History of Union County* is being presented to the public for the first time in over fifty years. I am sure it will become a cherished volume for all who obtain a copy. They will enjoy the series much the same as those that cut and saved the feature almost three generations ago.

Dr. Neil Rosenstein

PROLOGUE

The teenager who created this newspaper series was in his final year at the Art Career School atop the Flatiron Building in Manhattan when the idea for *"The Illustrated History of Union County"* was born. He was an occasional reader of the *New York Journal American,* which ran the daily panel *"Your America Day by Day in Pictures,"* edited by Clark Kinnaird. It was a scholarly piece featuring graphics of the period to illustrate the text. The youth's idea was to take the concept and produce it in a comic book format, with original drawings to accompany the wording. He had already done some comic book work and several illustrations for pulp magazines.

Senator Bob Crane, to whom this book is dedicated, was the publisher of *The Elizabeth Daily Journal.* He was enthusiastic about the proposal to have the comic as a daily feature. The series began January 8, 1950, and ran in 173 editions. The project enjoyed the endorsement of Dr. Arthur L. Johnson, the superintendent of the Union County schools.

While the Newark and Rahway libraries were excellent research sources, the Elizabeth library with its comprehensive picture files, and its very helpful and enthusiastic staff, deserve an extra nod of appreciation.

The late Charles Philhower, celebrated author and historian, graciously allowed the cartoonist into his home and was very supportive. The historic accounts of Lee and Hetfield were an indispensable resource. Author and historian R. V. Hoffman so kindly allowed his *Unknown Soldier of Springfield* to be included in the series.

The superb published work of Alex Raymond, of *Flash Gordon* fame, Harold Foster, artist of *Prince Valiant*, and Neil O'Keefe, illustrator of *Dick's Adventures in Dreamland* greatly influenced the young cartoonist.

THE ILLUSTRATED HISTORY OF UNION County...

by FRANK HOWE

TO BEGIN THE STORY OF OUR COUNTY WE TURN THE CLOCK BACK *SIXTY MILLION YEARS!* AT THAT TIME THE AREA WAS AT THE BOTTOM OF A VAST OCEAN, INFESTED WITH *STRANGE SEA CREATURES.*

THE SEAS GRADUALLY RECEDED, THEN *CATACLYSMIC UPHEAVALS* FORMED THE WATCHUNG MOUNTAIN RANGE.

SOON THE LAND BECAME A *PRIMEVAL JUNGLE.*

AS RECENTLY AS *ONE MILLION BC* A GREAT GLACIER COVERED UNION COUNTY; OFTEN OFTEN *THREE MILES HIGH!*

DURING THIS PERIOD OF LIFE THERE IS EVIDENCE THAT *DINOSAURS* ROAMED THE FORESTS OF UNION COUNTY. GIANT *MAMMOTHS, MASTODONS,* AND FEROCIOUS *PECCARIES* WERE FOUND IN THIS AREA IN THOSE ANCIENT TIMES. THROUGH COUNTLESS AGES THE REGION KNEW ONLY THESE ABORIGINAL INHABITANTS. THEN, MILLIONS OF YEARS AFTER THE MONSTERS HAD VANISHED A *TINY WHITE SAIL* APPEARED ON THE HORIZON, AND A *NEW ERA* HAD BEGUN!

THE ILLUSTRATED HISTORY OF UNION County...

by FRANK DHOTWE

1609

ON THE SIXTH OF SEPTEMBER, 395 YEARS AGO, THE SHIP *HALF MOON*, WITH A CREW OF TWENTY STALWART SEAMEN FROM THE OLD WORLD, SIGHTED LAND.

PRESENT SITE OF U.C. COURT HOUSE → IN ELIZABETH

UNION COUNTY, ALL MAP AREA VAST WILDERNESS

BAYONNE

BROOKLYN

STATEN ISLAND

SOUTH AMBOY

HENRY HUDSON, THE CAPTAIN OF THE VESSEL, WAS COMMISSIONED BT THE EAST INDIA COMPANY OF THE UNITED PROVINCES TO FIND A ROUTE TO CHINA, BUT INSTEAD HE SAILED INTO *SANDY HOOK BAY*, (ARROW AT LEFT), AND CAST ANCHOR.

THE NEXT DAY THE NATIVES VISITED THE BOAT. THEY WERE GLAD TO SEE THE WHITE MEN. HUDSON TRADED WITH THEM AND LEARNED OF THEIR HABITS AND WAYS OF LIFE. MEANWHILE, SOME OF THE CREW WERE EXPLORING THE LAND.

UNION County...

by FRANK THORNE

1609

THE MORNING AFTER THE HALF MOON ARRIVED IN SANDY HOOK BAY HENRY HUDSON SENT *JOHN COLEMAN* AND FOUR CREWMEN TO EXPLORE THE HARBOR. THEY SAILED UP THE ARTHUR KILL TO WHAT IS NOW *ELIZABETHPORT* (X ON MAP).

NOTE: UNION COUNTY WAS ACTUALLY FORMED IN 1857, BUT WE WILL REFER TO THE AREA AS IT IS KNOWN TO US TODAY.

SUNDAY, THE SIXTH OF SEPTEMBER, 1609, THE FIRST WHITE MEN SET FOOT IN UNION COUNTY. THEY STEPPED ASHORE AND MADE CONTACT WITH THE INDIANS AND LEARNED THAT THE AREA WAS KNOWN TO THE NATIVE POPULATION AS *SCHEYICHBI*, OR 'THE LAND OF THE SHELL WAMPUM.' THEY TOOK NOTE OF THE BEAUTIFUL COUNTRYSIDE AND BEGAN TO DEPART. JOHN COLEMAN (SPEAKING TO THE INDIANS ABOVE) WAS *SLAIN* BY THE TREACHEROUS ARROW OF A NATIVE BECAUSE HE HAD BROUGHT NO GIFTS!

THE ILLUSTRATED HISTORY OF UNION County...

by FRANK HOWE

1643

BEFORE THE SETTLEMENT OF UNION COUNTY THIS AREA WAS SPARSELY INHABITED BY THE *LENNI LENAPE*, MEANING 'REAL MEN' OR 'MEN AMONG MEN' IN THE NATIVE LANGUAGE.

THE LENAPE WERE A SMALL TRIBE OF SEVERAL THOUSAND THAT WERE DISPERSED THROUGHOUT NEW JERSEY.

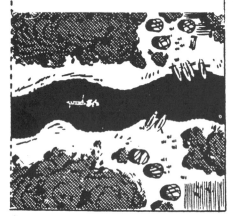

THEY WERE PART OF THE ALGONQUIAN TRIBAL CONFEDERACY CENTERED IN THE DELAWARE BASIN.

IN THE YEAR 1643 THE DUTCH MASSACRED EIGHTY OF THE UNSUSPECTING NATIVES AT WHAT IS NOW JERSEY CITY.

THE INDIANS IN TURN ATTACKED THE DUTCH SETTLEMENTS IN THE AREA OF *PRESENT DAY HOBOKEN* AND NEARBY *STATEN ISLAND*. AS TIME WENT ON THERE WERE ISOLATED INCIDENTS OF INDIAN UNREST IN UNION COUNTY. *THE FINAL CLASH TOOK PLACE IN THE EARLY 1700'S ON THE MINISINK TRAIL NEAR WHAT IS NOW NOMAHEGAN PARK IN CRANFORD.*

THE ILLUSTRATED HISTORY OF UNION County...

by FRANK THORNE

1633

BEFORE THE FIRST ENGLISH SETTLEMENTS IN NEW JERSEY THE DUTCH HAD ESTABLISHED PLANTATIONS IN WHAT IS NOW HUDSON COUNTY. THIS LAND WAS CONTROLLED BY WEALTHY DUTCH *PATROONS.*

A GROUP OF ENGLISH PLANTERS FROM LONG ISLAND TRIED TO OBTAIN A GRANT IN JERSEY FROM THE DUTCH AT NEW AMSTERDAM IN THE YEAR 1633.

BUT THE DUTCH DEMANDS WERE TOO HIGH AND NO AGREEMENT COULD BE MADE.

1664

DURING THE DUTCH SETTLEMENT OF THE NEW YORK AREA THE ENGLISH POURED INTO NEW ENGLAND. CONFLICTS OVER BOUNDARIES LED TO THE CAPTURE BY THE ENGLISH OF ALL THE DUTCH CONTROLLED LAND.

UNDER THE NEW ENGLISH RULE THE LONG ISLAND PLANTERS OBTAINED A GRANT FROM GOVERNOR NICHOLLS OF NEW YORK. ON STATEN ISLAND THE PURCHASE WAS MADE FROM SAGAMORE CHIEF MATTANO FOR ARTICLES VALUED AT *THREE HUNDRED AND SIXTY FIVE DOLLARS!*

WHITE AREA ON MAP INDICATES PURCHASE.

THE ILLUSTRATED HISTORY OF UNION County...

by FRANK SHOW

1664

AT ELIZABETHTOWN 'POINT' 341 YEARS AGO THERE WERE SOME *SIXTY FAMILIES* IN THE GROUP THAT HAD MIGRATED FROM LONG ISLAND AND CONNECTICUT.

ALL OF UNION COUNTY WAS A VAST WILDERNESS; AN UNSPOILED KINGDOM OF NATURE.

WITH LITTLE MORE THAN INDIAN PATHS TO FOLLOW THE PIONEERS FOUND THE *RIVER* THE ONLY PRACTICAL WAY TO EXPLORE THE SURROUNDING AREA.

THE CREEK (ELIZABETH RIVER)

PRESENT SITE OF COUNTY COURT HOUSE

THE FIRST ENGLISH COLONY IN N.J.

ELIZABETH PORT

STATEN ISLAND

ARTHUR KILL

THIS AERIAL VIEW OF THE ELIZABETH AREA IN 1664 SHOWS THE *FIRST ENGLISH COLONY* IN NEW JERSEY. THE SITE WAS AN *OLD INDIAN VILLAGE* AT THE MOUTH OF THE ELIZABETH RIVER. THE SETTLERS FIRST CONCERNS WERE FOOD AND REFUGE, SO THEY CONSTRUCTED SHELTERS SIMILAR TO THE INDIAN HUTCH (SEE PAGE 4), AND PLANTED GRAIN AND OTHER CROPS. THE ANNOYING MOSQUITOES IN THE UNDESIRABLE LOWLANDS FORCED THE SETTLERS TO MOVE UPSTREAM.

THE ILLUSTRATED HISTORY OF UNION County...

by FRANK HOWE

1665

THE TINY BAND OF PIONEERS HELD FAST ALONG THE ELIZABETH RIVER. THE STANDARD OF LIVING WAS *CRUDE* AND *EXTREMELY ELEMENTARY*, BUT THEY BRAVELY FOUGHT THE COLD AND DAMPNESS AS THE MONTHS DRAGGED ON.

IN SUCH AN ISOLATED FRONTIER THE SETTLERS EXISTENCE WAS MUCH LIKE THE NATIVE INDIAN.

THEY GATHERED FOOD AND SOME OF THEIR CLOTHING FROM THE FOREST AND THE RIVER; HUNTING THE SURROUNDING AREA TO PROVIDE MEAT FOR SUSTENANCE.

FORTUNATELY THE DEMANDS OF THIS PRIMITIVE LIFESTYLE WERE FEW AND READILY SATISFIED BY NATURE'S BOUNTY.

EACH FAMILY WOULD CLEAR A SMALL PLOT OF LAND AND PLANT AN ASSORTMENT OF VEGETABLES ALONG WITH *INDIAN CORN* WHICH WAS A STAPLE OF THEIR BASIC BUT NUTRITIOUS DIET. ONCE ESTABLISHED, THE RESOURCEFUL SETTLERS WOULD CLEAR MORE LAND FOR CROP GROWING. *AGRICULTURE* HAD BECOME UNION COUNTY'S *FIRST INDUSTRY*.

THE ILLUSTRATED HISTORY OF UNION County...

by FRANK THORNE

1665

THE NEW SETTLEMENT WAS UNDERWAY, EVER MORE LAND WAS CLEARED ALONG THE ELIZABETH RIVER, WHICH THE PIONEERS FONDLY CALLED 'THE CREEK'. THEY HELD REGULAR GROUP MEETINGS TO DISCUSS AFFAIRS OF THE DAY.

THE ANIMALS BECAME DOUBLY ALERT TO ELUDE THE NEW WHITE HUNTERS.

STEADY PROGRESS WAS MADE IN THE FIRST YEAR. THE INDIAN HUTCH-STYLE WAS REPLACED BY CRUDE LOG CABINS. LARGER BUILDINGS FOLLOWED, AND THE COMMUNITY PROSPERED.

EARLY IN AUGUST, 1665, ONE YEAR AFTER THE FIRST SIXTY FAMILIES ARRIVED, THERE WAS MUCH EXCITEMENT AT ELIZABETH POINT. *PHILIP CARTERET*, THE NEW GOVERNOR OF NEW JERSEY, HAD COME TO MAKE HIS RESIDENCE IN THE GROWING SETTLEMENT.

CARTERET NAMED THE NEW SETTLEMENT *'ELIZABETHTOWN'* IN HONOR OF ELIZABETH, WIFE OF SIR GEORGE CARTERET, WHO WAS THE PROPRIETARY LORD OF NEW JERSEY AND PHILIP'S COUSIN. THE NEW GOVERNOR DESIGNATED ELIZABETHTOWN AS THE *FIRST CAPITOL OF NEW JERSEY.* THIS AREA OF UNION COUNTY WAS HOST TO THE MOST IMPORTANT COLONY IN THE FLEDGLING STATE AT THAT TIME!

THE ILLUSTRATED HISTORY OF
UNION County...
by FRANK HOLME

1666

AS THE SETTLEMENT GREW, AN INCREASING NEED FOR HOUSEHOLD ARTICLES EVOLVED. COMMON ITEMS LIKE TABLES AND CHAIRS HAD TO BE HAND-CRAFTED BY THE COLONISTS.

FURNITURE WAS CONSTRUCTED FROM WOOD GATHERED FROM THE SURROUNDING FOREST.

THEIR PLATES AND OTHER SMALL RECEPTACLES WERE FASHIONED FROM FLAT STONES AND HOLLOWED-OUT GOURDS.

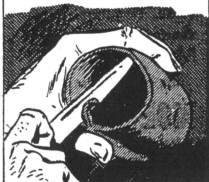

LARGE CONTAINERS WERE OFTEN CRAFTED FROM HOLLOW TREE STUMPS.

A ROARING FIREPLACE WAS A WELCOME SIGHT ON A CHILLY NIGHT IN THE COLONISTS' HOMES. THE SIZEABLE FIREPLACES WERE THE CENTER OF FAMILY LIFE IN THE WINTERTIME. ROOTED DEEP IN THE SOIL OF UNION COUNTY ARE THE SPIRITS OF THESE FIRST SETTLERS. IT IS WELL TO BRUSH BACK THE VEIL OF TIME AND CONTEMPLATE THEIR COMPARATIVELY SIMPLE HAPPY LIVES!

THE ILLUSTRATED HISTORY OF UNION County...

by FRANK THORNE

THE EARLY SETTLERS WERE OF THE MOST PART GOD-FEARING CHRISTIANS OF PURITAN PRINCIPLES. IN 1664 THE FIRST CONGREGATIONS WERE FORMED, MEETING IN ANY AVAILABLE HOME OR BARN.

IN 1666 THE GROWING NEED FOR A CHURCH BUILDING WAS MET. IT WAS CONSTRUCTED OF LOGS AND STOOD ON BROAD STREET WHERE THE FIRST PRESBYTERIAN CHURCH STANDS TODAY. AT FIRST IT WAS A NON-DENOMINATIONAL UNION CHURCH. THERE WERE NO PERMANENT MINISTERS IN THE AREA UNTIL 1668. IN THE INTERIM VISITING PASTORS CONDUCTED SERVICES IN THE NEW CHURCH. THE STRUCTURE BECAME *THE FIRST STATE CAPITOL BUILDING IN NEW JERSEY!* IN 1668 *THE FIRST STATE LEGISLATURE MET UNDER ITS ROOF* AS WAS *THE FIRST SESSION OF THE SUPREME COURT!* IN THE EARLY 1700'S THE HISTORIC STRUCTURE BECAME THE FIRST PRESBYTERIAN CHURCH OF ELIZABETHTOWN.

THE ILLUSTRATED HISTORY OF UNION County...

by FRANK THORNE

1680

IN THE SEVEN YEARS THAT *PHILIP CARTERET LIVED IN ELIZABETHTOWN BITTERNESS GREW BETWEEN THE GOVERNOR AND THE PEOPLE.

CARTERET'S CORRUPTION MOUNTED. HE LEVIED TAXES ON THE SOIL AND BEGAN TO MAKE GIFTS OF LAND TO HIS PERSONAL FRIENDS. THEN A SMALL GROUP OF SETTLERS MET AND DECIDED TO ACT. THEY RAIDED THE HOMES OF CARTERET'S CRONIES.

CARTERET TRIED TO PROSECUTE THE INSURGENTS, BUT THE RISING TIDE OF ANGER LEFT HIM POWERLESS. HE RETURNED TO ENGLAND AND REMAINED FOR TWO YEARS. CARTERET THEN CAME BACK TO ELIZABETHTOWN WHERE HE MET *A FITTING END TO HIS AUTOCRATIC CAREER*, AS WE SHALL SEE IN THE NEXT EPISODE.

DURING CARTERET'S REIGN A *WHALING COMPANY* WAS ORGANIZED IN ELIZABETHTOWN. AT THAT TIME WHALES WERE IN GREAT ABUNDANCE ALL ALONG THE NEW JERSEY COAST. THE COMPANY FLOURISHED, TAKING THE GREAT MAMMALS FROM THE WATERS OFF BARNEGAT BAY NORTH TO LOWER NEW YORK HARBOR. COMMERCIAL FISHING SOON BECAME AN IMPORTANT FACTOR IN THE LOCAL ECONOMY.

*A MORE COMPREHENSIVE ACCOUNT OF PHILIP CARTERET'S CONTROVERSIAL REIGN IS TOLD BEGINNING ON PAGE 91.

THE ILLUSTRATED HISTORY OF
UNION County...
by FRANK HOWE

1681

PHILIP CARTERET RETURNED TO NEW JERSEY FROM ENGLAND ONLY TO CONTINUE HIS DESPOTIC GOVERNORSHIP THEN, ONE DARK NIGHT, A GROUP OF MEN ENTERED HIS HOME IN ELIZABETHTOWN.

SIR EDMOND ANDROS, THE GOVERNOR OF NEW YORK, HAD ORDERED THAT CARTERET BE BROUGHT TO NEW YORK WHERE HE WAS BRUTALLY BEATEN AND IMPRISONED. ANDROS, WHO WAS AN EQUALLY GREEDY RULER, REMOVED CARTERET SO THAT HE MIGHT TAKE CONTROL OF NEW JERSEY AND ITS TREMENDOUS COMMERCIAL POSSIBILITIES. ANDROS SOON ARRIVED AT ELIZABETHTOWN AND TRIED TO ASSUME THE REINS OF GOVERNMENT.

THE ILLUSTRATED HISTORY OF UNION County...

by FRANK THORNE

1685

IN NEW YORK PHILIP CARTERET WAS PLACED ON TRIAL *FOR EXCEEDING HIS POWER AS GOVERNOR OF NEW JERSEY.* AFTER A LONG COURT BATTLE CARTERET WAS ACQUITTED AND STRIPPED OF HIS AUTHORITY.

HE RETURNED TO ELIZABETH-TOWN A POWERLESS AND DIFFERENT MAN.

FORTUNATELY ANDROS' PLANNED CONQUEST OF THIS AREA *FAILED*...THE PEOPLE REJECTED HIS ADMINISTRATION.

CARTERET DIED IN 1682, PRESUMABLY FROM INJURIES HE RECEIVED FROM ANDROS' HENCHMEN. CARTERET'S REIGN OF SEVENTEEN YEARS WAS TYPICAL OF MANY EARLY ADMINISTRATIONS, WHERE THE RULER WENT AGAINST EVERY PRINCIPLE OF THE PEOPLE. AFTER CARTERET *ROBERT BARKLEY, A QUAKER, WAS APPOINTED GOVERNOR.*

1685
1-ELIZABETH
2-UNION
3-SCOTCH PLAINS
4-RAHWAY

QUAKER RULE ATTRACTED MANY OF THAT SECT TO THE *RAHWAY SECTION* (4), LATER MOVING ON TO *PLAINFIELD.* THE MAP SHOWS THE FIRST SETTLEMENT OF *ELIZABETH* (1), WHICH INCLUDED AREAS OF *WESTFIELD, LINDEN, ROSELLE,* AND *HILLSIDE.* THE DARK SHADING INDICATES THE APPROXIMATE DEGREE OF SETTLEMENT IN THE REGION.

THE ILLUSTRATED HISTORY OF UNION County...
by FRANK HOLMES

1685

THEIR IMMEDIATE NEEDS SUPPLIED, THE PEOPLE OF UNION COUNTY TOOK THE NEXT STEP IN INDUSTRY. *DAMS* WERE BUILT AND *MILLS* WERE CONSTRUCTED HOUSING SIMPLE MACHINERY FOR SAWING WOOD AND GRINDING GRAIN.

THE PARTIALLY CLEARED WOODLANDS RINGING THE VILLAGES BECAME HOME TO HERDS OF PIGS AND HORSES, WHICH WERE COMMON PROPERTY.

SHEEP WERE NOT ALLOWED TO FREELY ROAM FOR IN THE DEEPER FOREST LAY MANY DANGERS; CHIEF AMONG THEM *PACKS OF HUNGRY WOLVES!*

GROUPS POURED INTO UNION COUNTY IN EVER INCREASING NUMBERS. AMONG THEM *COOPERS, CARPENTERS,* AND *SHIPBUILDERS,* WHO FILLED THE VITAL NEED FOR CRAFTSMEN. AT THAT TIME THE ELIZABETH RIVER COULD ACCOMMODATE *SHIPS OF THIRTY AND FORTY TONS!* THEY COULD SAIL ALL THE WAY UP TO BROAD STREET FROM THE ARTHUR KILL. THE VESSELS WOULD BE LOADED WITH SHIPMENTS OF CATTLE AND PRODUCE DESTINED FOR PUBLIC MARKETS IN NEW YORK CITY.

THE ILLUSTRATED HISTORY OF UNION County...

by FRANK HOWE

1700

THE LOCAL *INNS* AND *TAVERNS* WERE IMPORTANT IN COLONIAL UNION COUNTY. THEY WERE THE CENTER OF SOCIAL AND POLITICAL LIFE IN THE SETTLEMENTS.

PEOPLE WOULD STOP AT THE INN TO GET THE LATEST NEWS.

LODGINGS WERE AVAILABLE FOR WEARY TRAVELERS, BUT THE INNKEEPERS KEPT A WARY EYE ON STRANGERS. THEY WERE ON THE LOOKOUT FOR *WRONGDOERS* AND *RUNAWAY SLAVES*.

ONE OR MORE OF THESE LEGENDARY GATHERING PLACES WERE FOUND IN MOST OF THE SETTLEMENTS IN THE AREA. *DRUNKENNESS* WAS *NOT TOLERATED*. A PENALTY FOR BEING INTOXICATED WAS *STRICTLY ENFORCED*. THE OFFENDER WAS FINED FIVE SHILLINGS, APPROXIMATELY $1.25 IN TODAY'S EXCHANGE, THE MONEY WAS TO BE ADDED TO THE POOR FUND. IF THE LAWBREAKER DIDN'T PAY THE FINE HE WAS PLACED IN THE STOCKS.

THE ILLUSTRATED HISTORY OF UNION County...

by FRANK "HOWE"

1708

IN THE YEAR 1708 A BRIGHT YOUNG PREACHER NAMED *JONATHAN DICKINSON* ARRIVED AT ELIZABETHTOWN. HE WOULD FULFILL GREAT EXPECTATIONS.

REVEREND DICKINSON BECAME THE INITIAL PASTOR OF THE FIRST PRESBYTERIAN CHURCH. HE SERVED IN THIS ROLE FOR NEARLY FORTY YEARS. DURING HIS PASTORATE HE WAS NOTED FOR WORK IN THE SERVICE OF GOD AND THE EDUCATION OF HIS FELLOW MAN. DICKINSON WAS SURELY ONE OF THE GREATEST MEN OF THE COLONIAL ERA.

IN THE YEAR 1746, AT THE CLIMAX OF HIS CAREER, REVEREND DICKINSON FORMED THE *FIRST COLLEGE OF NEW JERSEY;* A SEMINARY TO TEACH THE CHRISTIAN MINISTRY.

THE FIRST TERM OF THE NEW 'COLLEGE OF NEW JERSEY' WAS HELD AT THE DICKENSON HOME (IT STOOD ON PEARL STREET BETWEEN WASHINGTON AVENUE AND RACE STREET.) JONATHAN DICKINSON DIED FOUR MONTHS LATER, NEVER TO KNOW THE GROWTH OF HIS IDEA. THE BURGEONING CLASSES MOVED INTO THE OLD ACADEMY NEAR THE FIRST CHURCH WHERE THE INFAMOUS STATESMAN AND VICE PRESIDENT *AARON BURR* ATTENDED CLASSES. THE ORIGINAL 'COLLEGE OF NEW JERSEY' IS NOW KNOWN AS *PRINCETON UNIVERSITY!*

THE ILLUSTRATED HISTORY OF UNION County...

by FRANK HOWE

1717

THE FOUR MAIN SETTLEMENTS HAD BEEN ESTABLISHED BEFORE 1700. A TYPICAL FAMILY, THE BRYANTS, MOVED WEST IN 1717 TO SETTLE IN WHAT IS NOW SPRINGFIELD.

BRYANT WAS THE TYPICAL 'MAN OF THE HOUR', AS WAS THE HEAD OF THE SAYER FAMILY; BOTH STURDY PIONEERS THAT WE HONOR IN THESE PAGES.

THE SAYERS, AMONG OTHERS, ARRIVED IN THE SUMMIT AREA IN 1720.

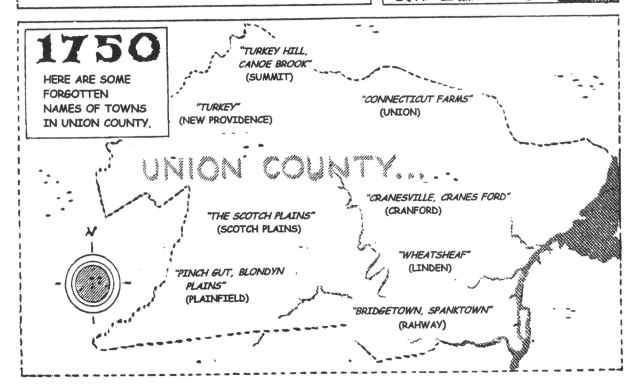

1750

HERE ARE SOME FORGOTTEN NAMES OF TOWNS IN UNION COUNTY.

"TURKEY HILL, CANOE BROOK" (SUMMIT)

"TURKEY" (NEW PROVIDENCE)

"CONNECTICUT FARMS" (UNION)

UNION COUNTY....

"CRANESVILLE, CRANES FORD" (CRANFORD)

"THE SCOTCH PLAINS" (SCOTCH PLAINS)

"WHEATSHEAF" (LINDEN)

N

"PINCH GUT, BLONDYN PLAINS" (PLAINFIELD)

"BRIDGETOWN, SPANKTOWN" (RAHWAY)

THE ILLUSTRATED HISTORY OF UNION County...
by FRANK THORNE

1750

GREAT CATTLE HERDS ABOUNDED IN UNION COUNTY AND THERE DEVELOPED AN INCREASING DEMAND FOR LEATHER; SO OF NECESSITY THE *TANNING INDUSTRY* WAS BORN.

TANNERIES BEGAN FULL SCALE PRODUCTION AND LEATHER WAS ADDED TO THE EXPORTS OF UNION COUNTY.

EVER BIGGER MANUFACTURERS WERE DRAWN TO THE AREA. PLANS FOR NEW MILLS WERE IMPLEMENTED. ELIZABETHTOWN HAD BECOME THE BOOMING *CULTURAL CENTER OF NEW JERSEY!*

THE AMAZING DEVELOPMENT OF UNION COUNTY IN THE EARLY 1700'S IS EXEMPLIFIED BY THE NUMBER OF MILLS THAT WERE BUILT. MOST EVERY VILLAGE HAD ONE OR MORE. *SPRINGFIELD,* AN IMPORTANT SETTLEMENT, HAD *TEN MILLS.* AMONG THEM WERE PAPER MILLS, ALONG WITH GRIST MILLS, SAW MILLS, AND FLOUR MILLS. SPRINGFIELD EVEN HOSTED A *TOBACCO FACTORY!*

THE ILLUSTRATED HISTORY OF UNION County...

by FRANK IHAW

1750

THE INDIAN DUGOUT WAS THE FIRST METHOD OF TRANSPORTATION, BUT IN THE 1700'S DIRT HIGHWAYS WERE DEVELOPED. HORSES AND OX CARTS WERE USED TO GET FROM ONE PLACE TO ANOTHER.

THEN AN EXCITING NEW VEHICLE APPEARED IN UNION COUNTY—THE *STAGECOACH!* ELIZABETHTOWN BECAME AN IMPORTANT STOP IN THE NETWORK OF STAGE ROUTES BETWEEN NEW YORK AND PHILADELPHIA.

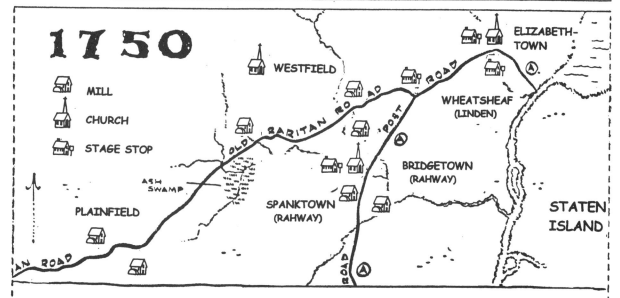

THIS MAP OF UNION COUNTY SHOWS *THE FIRST AND OLDEST ROAD IN NEW JERSEY.* (A) WHAT IS NOW *ST. GEORGES AVENUE* WAS OPENED BY THE DUTCH BEFORE THE ENGLISH SETTLEMENT (1664) TO MAINTAIN TRADE BETWEEN NEW AMSTERDAM AND THEIR COLONIES ON THE DELAWARE. OLD RARITAN ROAD (SHOWN ABOVE) WAS IN PLACE WELL BEFORE 1700.

THE ILLUSTRATED HISTORY OF UNION County...

by FRANK HOWE

1776

THIS ISSUE MARKS THE END OF THE *COLONIAL ERA* AND THE BEGINNING OF THE *REVOLUTIONARY PERIOD* IN UNION COUNTY.

FOR MANY YEARS THE COLONIES OPPOSED THE RULE OF ENGLAND.

THE NEWS OF *BUNKER HILL* AND THE *STAMP ACT* BEGAN TO AROUSE THE POPULACE.

SIDES WERE TAKEN IN THE GATHERING STORM. THE PATRIOTS, OR *WHIGS* WHO WANTED INDEPENDENCE FROM THE MOTHER COUNTRY, OPPOSED THE CONSERVATIVES, OR *TORIES*, WHO DIDN'T APPROVE OF THE CHANGE.

JUST BEFORE THE DECLARATION OF INDEPENDENCE WAS SIGNED IN 1776, THERE WERE SMALL GROUPS OF TORIES IN UNION COUNTY. IT WAS AT THIS TIME THAT THE PATRIOTS ERECTED A *GALLOWS IN ELIZABETHTOWN* (ON BROAD STREET). THEY LET IT BE KNOWN THAT ANYONE WHO POSSESSED OR DISTRIBUTED *STAMPED PAPER WOULD BE HUNG WITHOUT BENEFIT OF JUDGE OR JURY!*

THE ILLUSTRATED HISTORY OF UNION County...

by FRANK THORNE

1776

THE EXPECTED MOMENT HAD ARRIVED. *THE DECLARATION OF INDEPENDENCE* HAD BEEN SIGNED! *THE WAR WAS ON,* AND THE PATRIOTS PREPARED TO DEFEND UNION COUNTY.

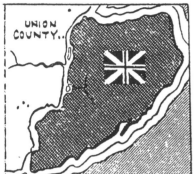

UNION COUNTY...

SUDDENLY ALL STATEN ISLAND FELL UNDER BRITISH CONTROL! MANY TORIES FLED TO THE ISLAND FROM UNION COUNTY.

THEN ELIZABETHTOWN POINT WAS FIRED ON BY ADVANCING BRITISH TROOPS! THE LOCAL MILITIA RACED TO THE SCENE AND REPELLED THE ATTACK.

PREPARATIONS WERE MADE FOR WAR IN THE SUCCEEDING MONTHS. NEWS REACHED THE PATRIOTS THAT *NEW YORK HAD FALLEN TO THE BRITISH,* AND GENERAL WASHINGTON, WITH HIS DEPLETED ARMY, WAS RETREATING SOUTH THROUGH NEW JERSEY. THEIR ARRIVAL IN ELIZABETHTOWN WAS IMMINENT. THE ENEMY WAS IN CLOSE PURSUIT, SO THE ORDER WAS GIVEN TO *EVACUATE!*

THE ILLUSTRATED HISTORY OF
UNION County...
by FRANK HOWE

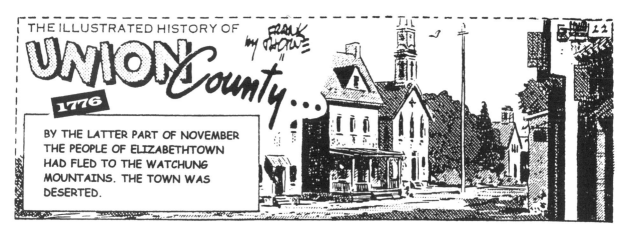

1776

BY THE LATTER PART OF NOVEMBER THE PEOPLE OF ELIZABETHTOWN HAD FLED TO THE WATCHUNG MOUNTAINS. THE TOWN WAS DESERTED.

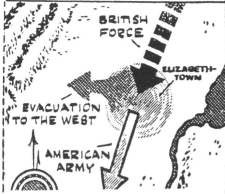

BRITISH FORCE

ELIZABETH-TOWN

EVACUATION TO THE WEST

AMERICAN ARMY

WASHINGTON'S ARMY RETREATED THROUGH ELIZABETHTOWN, HEADING SOUTH TOWARD NEW BRUNSWICK.

THE MILITIA MADE CAMP NEAR SHORT HILLS AND PLANNED THEIR DEFENSE STRATEGY.

IN THOSE DARK DAYS SOME OF THE PATRIOTS TURNED *TRAITOR* AND JOINED THE ENEMY THINKING THE REBEL CAUSE WAS LOST.

ON NOVEMBER 29TH, 1776, THE REDCOATS OCCUPIED ELIZABETHTOWN. THEY RAVAGED THE HOMES AND TOOK A GREAT QUANTITY OF STORES. THE BRITISH ISSUED A PROCLAMATION TO 'ALL PERSONS WHO TOOK UP ARMS AGAINST THE KING' TO RETURN HOME AND BE GRANTED A FULL PARDON. MEANWHILE, WASHINGTON'S ARMY CONTINUED TO RETREAT. *ALL SEEMED LOST!*

THE ILLUSTRATED HISTORY OF UNION County...

by FRANK THORNE

1776

THE DISPLACED PATRIOT FAMILIES BECAME INCREASINGLY DISCOURAGED KNOWING THEIR HOMES WERE BEING PILLAGED BY THE OCCUPYING ARMY.

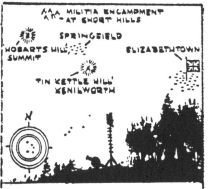

A WARNING CANNON AND TAR BARRELS ON TALL POLES WERE PUT IN PLACE TO AROUSE THE PEOPLE IN THE EVENT OF AN ATTACK.

ON DECEMBER 17TH A SMALL STATION OF MILITIA AT SPRINGFIELD SPOTTED A LARGE BRITISH FORCE ADVANCING WEST.

A HORSEMAN RACED TO CHATHAM TO SUMMON THE AMERICAN FORCES!

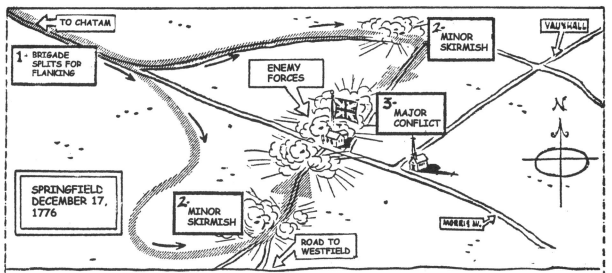

AS THE BRITISH OCCUPIED THE VILLAGE AN AMERICAN BRIGADE ADVANCED IN A FLANKING MANEUVER (1). THE MAJOR CONFLICT (3) LASTED ABOUT AN HOUR, THEN DARKNESS PUT AN END TO THE FIGHTING. DURING THE NIGHT THE BRITISH RETREATED BACK TO ELIZABETHTOWN, THIS SKIRMISH WAS A GREAT MORALE BUILDER, FOR IT WAS *THE FIRST TIME THE REDCOATS RETREATED IN NEW JERSEY,* PROVING THAT THEY WERE *NOT INVINCIBLE!*

THE ILLUSTRATED HISTORY OF UNION County...

by FRANK THORNE

ON DECEMBER 26TH, 1776, GENERAL WASHINGTON WON HIS *BRILLIANT VICTORY AT TRENTON*, CAPTURING *918 HESSIAN TROOPS!* THIS NEWS BROUGHT *NEW HOPE* TO THE PEOPLE OF UNION COUNTY.

Retreat of British...Jan.5.
- battle
- tavern
- church

Elizabeth-town

(LINDEN)

(ST. GEORGES AVE.)

river

(GIRL SCOUT HOUSE)

Spanktown (RAHWAY)

post road

(TO WESTFIELD)

(TO WOODBRIDGE)

THE REJUVENATED AMERICAN FORCES ATTACKED FROM NEWARK AND DROVE THE ENEMY SOUTH TO RAHWAY WHERE THEY TOOK A BRIEF STAND BEFORE RETREATING TO WOODBRIDGE,

IN THE SECOND WEEK OF JANUARY THE RESIDENTS OF ELIZABETHTOWN RETURNED TO THEIR HOMES. THEY FOUND EVERYTHING IN RUINS. HOUSES WERE PLUNDERED AND GARDENS LAID WASTE. MUCH OF THE DAMAGE WAS DONE BY THEIR *OWN TORY NEIGHBORS* WHO HAD VENTURED FROM THEIR REFUGE IN BRITISH-CONTROLLED STATEN ISLAND.

THE ILLUSTRATED HISTORY OF UNION County...

by FRANK THORNE

1777

FOR THE NEXT SIX MONTHS THE BRITISH ARMY WAS KEPT AT BAY IN THE WOODBRIDGE-AMBOY AREA. BUT THERE WERE CONSTANT ALARMS AS THE ENEMY VENTURED NORTH ON PROBING MISSIONS.

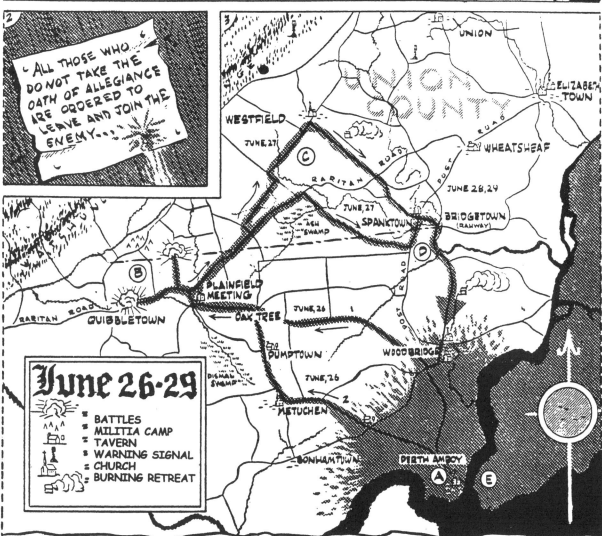

" ALL THOSE WHO DO NOT TAKE THE OATH OF ALLEGIANCE ARE ORDERED TO LEAVE AND JOIN THE ENEMY..."

June 26-29

- ☼ = BATTLES
- ⋀⋀⋀ = MILITIA CAMP
- 🏠 = TAVERN
- ⌂ = WARNING SIGNAL
- ⛪ = CHURCH
- = BURNING RETREAT

THE REDCOATS (A) MADE ONE LAST ATTEMPT TO CAPTURE WASHINGTON'S ARMY LOCATED IN THE HILLS TO THE NORTHWEST. TWO LARGE ENEMY COLUMNS ADVANCED TO PLAINFIELD (B) AND WERE TURNED BACK BY AMERICAN FORCES, ONE COLUMN REACHED WESTFIELD, THEN RETREATED TO RAHWAY (D). THEY SPENT THE NIGHT AND UPON HEARING OF ADVANCING AMERICAN FORCES THEY RETREATED TO AMBOY AND CROSSED TO STATEN ISLAND (E), *ENDING THEIR OCCUPATION OF NEW JERSEY.*

THE ILLUSTRATED HISTORY OF UNION County...

by FRANK THORNE

1777

THE PEOPLE OF UNION COUNTY TRIED TO RESUME A SOMEWHAT NORMAL LIFE, BUT THE ENEMY WAS STILL MASSED IN GREAT FORCE JUST ACROSS THE ARTHUR KILL ON NEARBY STATEN ISLAND.

A CONSTANT GUARD WAS KEPT ALL ALONG THE SHORELINE ON THE ALERT FOR ANOTHER INVASION.

STILL, THROUGHOUT THE DURATION OF THE WAR, THERE WERE CONTINUAL RAIDS ON ELIZABETHTOWN BY SMALL ENEMY GROUPS THAT INFILTRATED THE DEFENSE LINES.

DURING THIS PERIOD SOME OF THE LOCAL RESIDENTS CARRIED ON EXTENSIVE *TRADING WITH THE BRITISH!* THEIR TRAITOROUS BUSINESS WAS USUALLY CARRIED ON AT NIGHT TO AVOID DETECTION. IF THE CULPRITS WERE CAUGHT THEY WERE PUNISHED AS ENEMIES OF THE STATE.

THE ILLUSTRATED HISTORY OF UNION County...

by FRANK "HOWE"

1779

SHEPARD KOLLOCK, AN ENTERPRISING OFFICER IN WASHINGTON'S ARMY, WAS A PRINTER BY PROFESSION. HE WOULD PLAY A VITAL ROLE IN THE LIVES OF THE COUNTY'S RESIDENTS.

GENERAL WASHINGTON WAS INCENSED WITH THE TORY REPORTS IN THE *NEW YORK GAZETTE* THAT WAS BEING DISTRIBUTED THROUGHOUT NEW JERSEY.

WASHINGTON AND HIS OFFICERS RAISED THE MONEY FOR A NEWSPAPER OF THEIR OWN. KOLLOCK WAS PUT TO WORK. AT FIRST HIS PRESS WAS MOUNTED ON A WAGON SO HE COULD FOLLOW THE MOVEMENTS OF THE ARMY.

THE NEWSPAPER WAS TITLED *THE NEW JERSEY JOURNAL*, AND IT WAS WIDELY READ BY THE AMERICAN TROOPS AND THEIR FAMILIES NOT ONLY IN NEW JERSEY BUT MANY OF THE SURROUNDING NEW STATES. AFTER THE CONCLUSION OF HOSTILITIES KOLLOCK MOVED TO ELIZABETHTOWN WHERE HE CONTINUED TO PUBLISH THE PAPER. YES, THIS HISTORIC PUBLICATION WAS THE GREAT-GREAT-GRAND-DADDY OF *THE ELIZABETH DAILY JOURNAL*!

THE ILLUSTRATED HISTORY OF
UNION County...

by FRANK TROWE

28

THE YEARS 1778 AND 1779 FOUND THE COUNTY RESIDENTS STILL UNEASY WITH THE BRITISH PRESENCE ACROSS THE KILL. TO MAKE MATTERS WORSE THE WINTER OF 1780 WAS ONE OF THE MOST SEVERE ON RECORD.

ON THE NIGHT OF JUNE 7TH, 1780, A BRITISH FORCE OF *SIX THOUSAND REDCOATS* LED BY MAJOR GENERAL KNYPHAUSEN CROSSED THE RIVER AND ASSEMBLED AT ELIZABETHPORT. KNYPHAUSEN WAS DETERMINED TO MARCH ON MORRISTOWN AND CAPTURE WASHINGTON'S ARMY. *IT WAS TO BE ONE OF THE MOST MEMORABLE CAMPAIGNS OF THE WAR.*

THE ILLUSTRATED HISTORY OF UNION County...

by FRANK *"SHOW"*

BRITISH GENERAL *STIRLING* LED HIS TROOPS UP THE KING'S HIGHWAY (WHAT IS NOW FIRST AVENUE) IN ELIZABETHTOWN.

AN OUTPOST OF MEN FROM COL. ELIAS DAYTON'S BRIGADE SPOTTED THEM AT UNION SQUARE (WHERE THE STATUE OF THE MINUTE-MAN STANDS TODAY).

THEY BLASTED AWAY AT THE REDCOATS, BUT WERE SOON DRIVEN BACK. BUT DURING THE SKIRMISH...

STIRLING WAS *MORTALLY WOUNDED* BY A SHARP-SHOOTER IN DAYTON'S CONTINGENT!

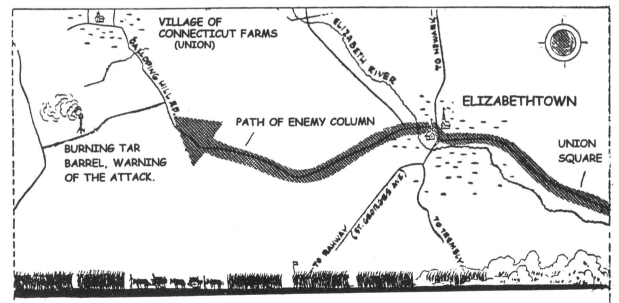

VILLAGE OF CONNECTICUT FARMS (UNION)

ELIZABETH RIVER

TO NEWARK

ELIZABETHTOWN

PATH OF ENEMY COLUMN

BURNING TAR BARREL, WARNING OF THE ATTACK.

UNION SQUARE

GALLOPING HILL RD.

TO RAHWAY (ST. GEORGES AVE)

TO TREMBLY

THE ENEMY COLUMN RESUMED ITS MARCH THROUGH ELIZABETHTOWN OUT WHAT IS NOW *WESTFIELD AVE* UP *GALLOPING HILL ROAD* TOWARD THE VILLAGE OF CONNECTICUT FARMS (UNION). THEY MET STINGING ATTACKS BY THE MINUTEMEN ALL ALONG THEIR ROUTE.

THE ILLUSTRATED HISTORY OF UNION County...

by FRANK HOWE

June 7, 1780

THE ALARM WAS SOUNDED! THE SIGNAL CANNON ON HOBART'S HILL *BOOMED* AND THE TAR BARREL WAS IGNITED. THE DRUMS IN THE MORRIS-TOWN ENCAMPMENT *BEAT TO ARMS.*

JUST OUTSIDE THE VILLAGE OF CONNECTICUT FARMS THE ENEMY COLUMN MET THE *FULL FORCE* OF DAYTON'S BRIGADE, THE MILITIA, AND JUST ABOUT *ANYONE WHO COULD FIRE A GUN!* THE *BATTLE WAS ON!* THE AMERICANS BLASTED AWAY AT THE LARGER FORCE FROM BEHIND EVERY TREE AND BUSH.

BRITISH GENERAL KNYPHAUSEN WAS AMAZED AT THE EFFICIENCY OF THE SHABBY AMERICAN FORCES. THE RESISTANCE WAS SUCH THAT THE ENRAGED GENERAL ORDERED HIS MEN RETREAT! WHEN THEY REACHED THE VILLAGE KNYPHAUSEN GAVE THE COMMAND *TO BURN THE SETTLEMENT TO THE GROUND.* THEN THE PLUNDERING BEGAN!

THE ILLUSTRATED HISTORY OF
UNION County...
by Frank Thorne

June 7, 1780

THE BRITISH AND HESSIAN SOLDIERS OBEYED THE ORDERS OF THEIR ENRAGED LEADER. AFTER PILLAGING THE HOMES THEY SET THEM ABLAZE. THEN THE RIOTOUS MOB APPROACHED THE CHURCH.

THE *WIFE OF REV. JAMES CALDWELL* WAS CARING FOR HER CHILDREN IN THE PARSONAGE BEHIND THE MAIN CHURCH BUILDING.

MRS. CALDWELL HAD BEEN WARNED OF THE ENEMY'S APPROACH, BUT SHE WAS CERTAIN THEY WERE NOT IN HARM'S WAY.

THEN SHE AND THE HOUSE-KEEPER HEARD THE ROWDY APPROACH OF THE BRITISH AND THEIR BRUTAL GERMAN MERCENARIES.

MRS. CALDWELL WENT TO THE WINDOW AND SAW A HESSIAN SOLDIER APPROACHING. THE HOUSE-KEEPER SCREAMED, BUT MRS. CALDWELL CALMLY ASSURED HER THAT EVERYTHING WOULD BE ALL RIGHT AND THAT GOD WOULD PROTECT THEM. SUDDENLY THE HESSIAN RAISED HIS MUSKET AND *FIRED POINT BLANK.* THE BULLET *KILLED HER INSTANTLY!*

THE ILLUSTRATED HISTORY OF UNION County...

by FRANK HOWE

June 7-23 1780

THEIR DIRTY WORK DONE, THE BEATEN REDCOATS RETREATED IN THE DARK OF NIGHT THROUGH A BLINDING RAINSTORM AND TOOK UP A DEFENSE POSITION BACK AT ELIZABETHPORT.

AFTER A CHECK OF CASUALTIES THE AMERICANS REPORTED ONLY EIGHT KILLED.

THE BRITISH TOOK HEAVY LOSSES, BUT THEY PLANNED ANOTHER ATTACK!

SIXTEEN DAYS LATER FIVE THOUSAND ENEMY TROOPS UNDER *SIR HENRY CLINTON* LEFT THE PORT AND MARCHED WEST. THEY REACHED THE BURNED OUT VILLAGE OF CONNECTICUT FARMS AT DAYBREAK.

THE AMERICAN FORCES SET UP A DEFENSE PERIMETER, THIS TIME AT—

Springfield...

AS THE ENEMY NEARED, SMALL ADVANCE STATIONS WERE PLACED AT THE BRIDGES ON THE APPROACH TO THE VILLAGE.

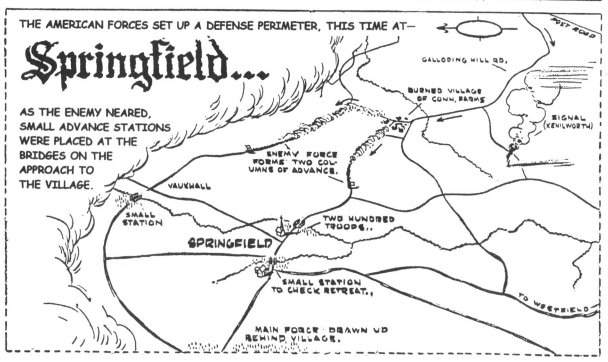

THE ILLUSTRATED HISTORY OF UNION County...

by FRANK HOLM

43

THE AMERICAN GUNS BLAZED AGAIN, AND *THE BATTLE FOR SPRINGFIELD BEGAN!*

DURING THE HEAT OF BATTLE A CRY WENT UP FOR WADDING FROM COL. DAYTON'S GROUP AT A BRIDGE NEAR THE CHURCH!

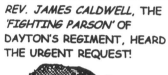

REV. JAMES CALDWELL, THE *'FIGHTING PARSON'* OF DAYTON'S REGIMENT, HEARD THE URGENT REQUEST!

WHERE WAS THE ALL-IMPORTANT *WADDING* TO COME FROM? SUDDENLY THE SOUND OF *HOOF BEATS* WAS HEARD!

PARSON CALDWELL CAME CRASHING THROUGH THE BRUSH WITH AN ARMFUL OF WATTS' HYMNALS HE HAD APPROPRIATED FROM THE NEARBY CHURCH! THE MEN COULD EASILY TEAR THE PAGES TO SIZE, ALLOWING THEM TO USE IT AS WADDING WHILE MUZZLE-LOADING THEIR MUSKETS. HE PASSED THE BOOKS OUT TO THE TROOPS SHOUTING *"NOW PUT WATTS INTO THEM BOYS!"* IT'S LIKELY THAT HIS FEAT OF BRAVERY WAS DONE TO AVENGE THE MURDER OF HIS WIFE SIXTEEN DAYS BEFORE!

THE ILLUSTRATED HISTORY OF UNION County...
by FRANK "HOW"

June 23, 1780

THE BRITISH DROVE BACK THE AMERICAN FORCES AND OCCUPIED THE VILLAGE OF SPRINGFIELD, BUT THEY PAID HEAVILY FOR THEIR VICTORY.

THEN AN ENEMY SCOUT CAME TO THE REDCOAT GENERAL WITH SOME DISTURBING NEWS.

AN OVERWHELMING FORCE OF WASHINGTON'S REJUVENATED ARMY HAD LEFT MORRISTOWN AND WAS APPROACHING FROM THE WEST!

THE REDCOATS TURNED AND RAN, BUT NOT BEFORE TORCHING MORE HOMES, SENDING SPIRALING COLUMNS OF SMOKE INTO THE COOL JUNE AIR. THE ENTIRE ENEMY FORCE RETREATED BACK TO ELIZABETHPORT AND CROSSED OVER TO STATEN ISLAND, ENDING THE MOST MEMORABLE CAMPAIGN IN THE HISTORY OF UNION COUNTY. THE PEOPLE RETURNED TO THEIR HOMES, AND SAVE FOR A FEW MINOR SKIRMISHES *THE FIGHTING WAS OVER!*

THE ILLUSTRATED HISTORY OF **UNION** *County...* by FRANK HOWE

Nov. 24, 1781

THE MYSTERIOUS CIRCUMSTANCES SURROUNDING THE DEATH OF THE MUCH BELOVED REVEREND CALDWELL CAME AS A GREAT SHOCK TO THE PEOPLE OF UNION COUNTY.

HE WAS WAITING FOR A MEMBER OF HIS FLOCK WHO WAS ARRIVING BY BOAT FROM NEW YORK.

AS HE ESCORTED HER TO HIS CARRIAGE AN AMERICAN SOLDIER STOPPED THEM AND INQUIRED ABOUT THE BUNDLE SHE WAS CARRYING.

THE SOLDIER SUSPECTED THE PACKAGE CONTAINED CONTRABAND GOODS, AND HE RUDELY INSISTED SHE OPEN THE PARCEL.

PARSON CALDWELL OBJECTED, DEMANDING TO SEE HIS COMMANDING OFFICER. THE SOLDIER BACKED OFF, BUT AS CALDWELL AND THE WOMAN WALKED TOWARD THE CARRIAGE THE SOLDIER, WITHOUT PROVOCATION, *SHOT THE HIGHLY RESPECTED MINISTER. HE COLLAPSED ON THE PIER—DEAD!* THE MURDERER WAS IMMEDIATELY APPREHENDED, BUT HE COULD GIVE NO REASON FOR HIS CRIMINAL ACT. THE NEWS TRAVELED FAST, BEYOND ELIZABETHTOWN TO ALL THE NEW COLONIES.

UNION County...

1783

THE TREATY OF PEACE WITH ENGLAND WAS SIGNED IN 1783. THE *HON. ELIAS BOUDINOT,* AN ELIZABETHTOWN RESIDENT, WAS ONE OF THE SIGNERS OF THE HISTORIC ACCORD. BOUDINOT WAS A MEMBER AND *PRESIDENT* OF THE *CONTINENTAL CONGRESS.*

by FRANK THORNE

AFTER *EIGHT LONG YEARS* THE WAR WAS OVER, AND THE TROOPS WERE COMING HOME!

THE BRAVERY OF THE NEW JERSEY MILITIA THROUGHOUT THE CONFLICT WAS OUTSTANDING. GENERAL WASHINGTON WROTE...

"THEY FLEW TO ARMS UNIVERSALLY, AND ACTED WITH A SPIRIT EQUAL TO ANYTHING I HAVE SEEN IN THE COURSE OF THE WAR."

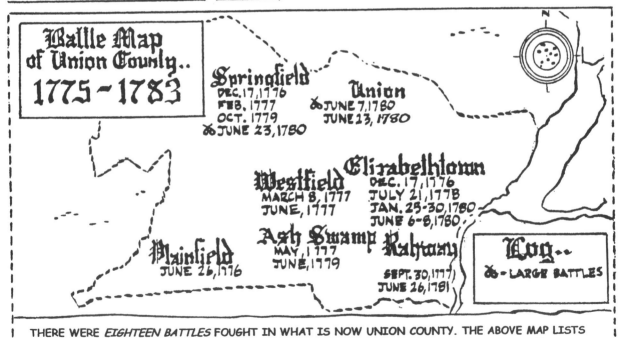

Battle Map of Union County.. 1775 ~ 1783

Springfield
DEC. 17, 1776
FEB. 1777
OCT. 1779
⚔ JUNE 23, 1780

Union
⚔ JUNE 7, 1780
JUNE 13, 1780

Westfield
MARCH 8, 1777
JUNE, 1777

Elizabethtown
DEC. 17, 1776
JULY 21, 1778
JAN. 25-30, 1780
JUNE 6-8, 1780

Ash Swamp
MAY, 1777
JUNE, 1779

Rahway
SEPT. 30, 1777
JUNE 26, 1781

Plainfield
JUNE 26, 1776

Log..
⚔ = LARGE BATTLES

THERE WERE *EIGHTEEN BATTLES* FOUGHT IN WHAT IS NOW UNION COUNTY. THE ABOVE MAP LISTS THE LOCATIONS AND DATES OF THE CLASHES BETWEEN THE BRITISH AND AMERICAN FORCES.

THE ILLUSTRATED HISTORY OF UNION County...

by FRANK

1789

UNION COUNTY, BEING IN SUCH A STRATEGIC POSITION DURING THE HOSTILITIES, HAD FREQUENT VISITS BY GENERAL WASHINGTON. THE MOST MOMENTOUS WAS HIS STOP AT ELIZABETHTOWN IN 1789.

WASHINGTON LEFT NEW BRUNSWICK HEADING FOR NEW YORK CITY FOR HIS *INAUGURATION.*

HE WAS TO BECOME THE *FIRST PRESIDENT OF THE UNITED STATES!* HE WAS MET BY CHEERING CROWDS ALONG THE WAY.

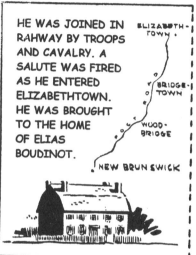

HE WAS JOINED IN RAHWAY BY TROOPS AND CAVALRY. A SALUTE WAS FIRED AS HE ENTERED ELIZABETHTOWN. HE WAS BROUGHT TO THE HOME OF ELIAS BOUDINOT.

WASHINGTON WAS GRACIOUSLY RECEIVED AT THE BOUDINOT HOME (1073 E. JERSEY ST.) BY A COMMITTEE OF CONGRESS, AND ENTERTAINED BY *ELIAS BOUDINOT* (ABOVE ON WASHINGTON'S LEFT) AT A TWO-HOUR LUNCHEON. OTHER PROMINENT GUESTS INCLUDED *GOVERNOR LIVINGSTON* (BEHIND WASHINGTON), *JOHN JAY, JOHN LANGDON* AND OTHER NOTABLES. AFTER THE GATHERING THE PRESIDENT-ELECT DEPARTED FOR NEW YORK BY BOAT FROM ELIZABETHPORT.

THE ILLUSTRATED HISTORY OF UNION County...
by FRANK HOWE

1800

AS THE COUNTY'S VILLAGES GREW TO BECOME SELF-SUSTAINING COMMUNITIES, MANY INDUSTRIES BEGAN TO FLOURISH.

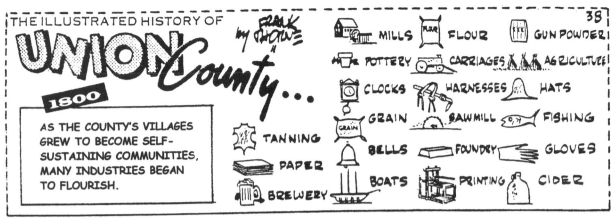

MILLS · FLOUR · GUN POWDER
POTTERY · CARRIAGES · AGRICULTURE
CLOCKS · HARNESSES · HATS
GRAIN · SAWMILL · FISHING
BELLS · FOUNDRY · GLOVES
BOATS · PRINTING · CIDER
TANNING · PAPER · BREWERY

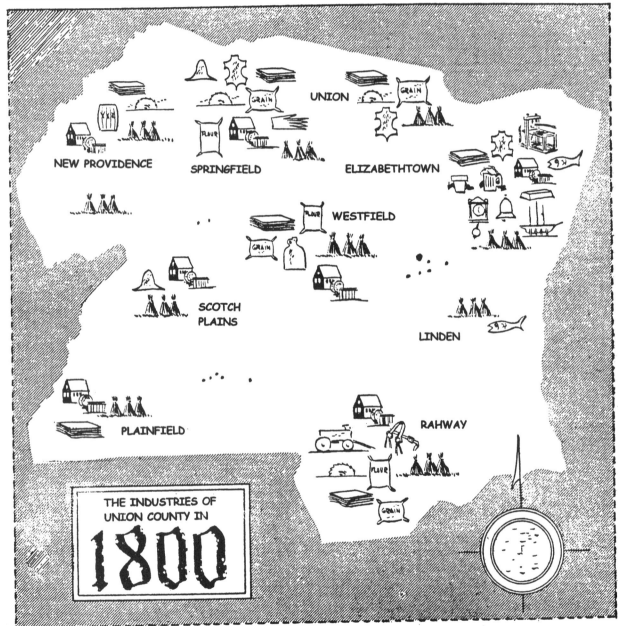

NEW PROVIDENCE

SPRINGFIELD

UNION

ELIZABETHTOWN

WESTFIELD

SCOTCH PLAINS

LINDEN

PLAINFIELD

RAHWAY

THE INDUSTRIES OF UNION COUNTY IN

1800

THE ILLUSTRATED HISTORY OF

UNION County...

by FRANK THORNE

1800

ELIZABETHTOWN, FROM THE EARLY DAYS, MAINTAINED A *FERRY SERVICE* TO STATEN ISLAND AND NEW YORK CITY. AT FIRST IT WAS A *DUGOUT CANOE*, BUT IN 1800...

...A TRAVELER WOULD COME TO ELIZABETHPORT AND ARRANGE PASSAGE.

TO PASS THE TIME BEFORE DEPARTING, THE TAVERN AT THE 'POINT' PROVIDED REFRESHMENT.

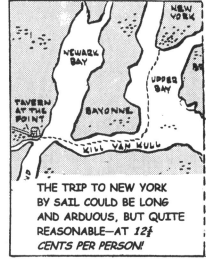

THE TRIP TO NEW YORK BY SAIL COULD BE LONG AND ARDUOUS, BUT QUITE REASONABLE—AT *12½ CENTS PER PERSON!*

THE PEOPLE OF UNION COUNTY HAD HEARD OF *ROBERT FULTON* AND HIS STEAMBOAT. THEN ONE EXCITING DAY THE LOCALS THRONGED TO THE POINT AND BEHELD THE NEW FERRY RUN BY *STEAM POWER!* SOON NEW REGULAR FERRY SCHEDULES WERE MAINTAINED. IN 1811, THE 'SEA HORSE' BEGAN HER PROUD SERVICE WHICH LASTED MANY LONG YEARS. THE FERRY RIDES TO NEW YORK HAD BECOME MUCH FASTER AND A LOT LESS GRUELING.

THE ILLUSTRATED HISTORY OF UNION County...
by FRANK HOWE

THE YEAR 1812 SAW THE YOUNG COUNTRY PLUNGE INTO A NEW WAR WITH ENGLAND. THIS TIME OVER DEFIANCE TO BRITISH SUPREMACY OF THE SEAS. MANY COUNTY MEN JOINED THE FIGHTING.

THE WAR ENDED IN 1815, WHICH INITIATED A TREMENDOUS ERA OF PROGRESS AND PROSPERITY IN UNION COUNTY. SIGNIFICANTLY, IN 1834, A BAND OF WORKMEN LAID A NARROW, SINGLE RAILROAD TRACK ON THE VAST FARMLANDS OF THE AREA, THE ROUTE FOLLOWS THE SAME ROADBED AS THE TRACKS OF THE PENNSYLVANIA RAILROAD, HOME TO NEW JERSEY TRANSIT,

WHEN THE FIRST *STEAM TRAINS* CAME CHUGGING AND PUFFING THROUGH ELIZABETHTOWN THE RESIDENTS WERE FASCINATED, SOME LAUGHED, OTHERS BECAME FRIGHTENED. IT WAS REPORTED THAT SEVERAL LADIES FAINTED AWAY AT THE SIGHT! THE LITTLE NARROW GAUGE GREW MIGHTILY, TO BECOME A VITAL PART OF THE COUNTY'S ECONOMY. BY 1840 THE TRACKS REACHED *PHILADELPHIA*. IN 1840 A TRACK CONNECTED ELIZABETHTOWN WITH *SOMERVILLE*. SOON THE *WHOLE COUNTRY* WOULD BE LINKED BY RAIL.

THE ILLUSTRATED HISTORY OF UNION County...

by FRANK THORNE

County seal

1857

41

Rein

SEAL OF THE COUNTY OF UNION • NEW JERSEY • 1857

ON APRIL 13TH, 1857, UNION COUNTY WAS *OFFICIALLY FORMED* FROM THE SOUTHERN SECTION OF ESSEX COUNTY. THE OFFICIAL SEAL WAS DESIGNED. DEPICTED ON IT IS THE *MURDER OF REV. JAMES CALDWELL'S WIFE* AT SPRINGFIELD A CENTURY BEFORE.

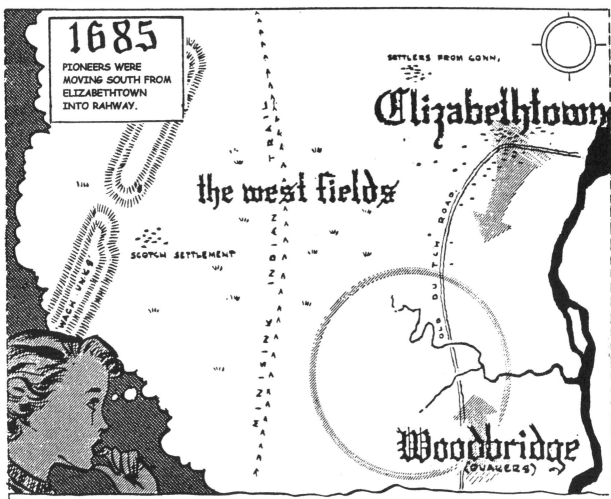

1685

PIONEERS WERE MOVING SOUTH FROM ELIZABETHTOWN INTO RAHWAY.

SETTLERS FROM CONN,

Elizabethtown

the west fields

SCOTCH SETTLEMENT

MINISINK TRAIL

WACH UNKS

OLD DUTCH ROAD

Woodbridge (QUAKERS)

WITH THE FORMATION OF UNION COUNTY ENDS THE FIRST SECTION OF THIS SERIES. THE SECOND SECTION WILL FEATURE A *DETAILED PICTORIAL HISTORY OF INDIVIDUAL MAIN SETTLEMENT AREAS. RAHWAY* WILL BE CONSIDERED FIRST, FOLLOWED BY PLAINFIELD, WESTFIELD AND SO ON. NOW, *THROUGH YOUR IMAGINATION*, WITH THE HELP OF THE ILLUSTRATIONS AND TEXT, WE WILL JOURNEY BACK THROUGH TIME TO 1665 TO THE SHORES OF THE RAHWACK RIVER (CIRCLE ON MAP), WHERE A TINY SETTLEMENT HAS BEEN ESTABLISHED...

THE ILLUSTRATED HISTORY OF UNION County...
Rahway
by FRANK "THORN"

SOON AFTER 1664, PIONEERS MOVED SOUTH FROM ELIZABETHTOWN AND BEGAN SETTLING LOWER RAHWAY (A). THE NEXT YEAR, IN ORDER TO ESCAPE RELIGIOUS INTOLERANCE, A GROUP OF QUAKERS MOVED NORTH FROM WOODBRIDGE INTO THE RAHWAY AREA.

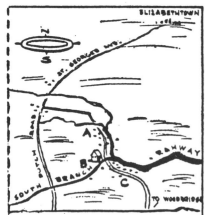

THE QUAKERS SETTLED ON THE SOUTH SHORE OF THE LOWER RAHWAY RIVER (C).

THEY FOUND A SIZABLE SETTLEMENT WITH A SAW MILL GOING FULL BLAST, TURNING OUT LUMBER FOR NEW HOMES.

EARLY ON, THE PEOPLE OF RAHWAY TRAVELED ALL THE WAY TO ELIZABETHTOWN TO WORSHIP.

THEN, IN 1741, AN INSPIRED PRESBYTERIAN GROUP FROM RAHWAY, MEMBERS OF REV. JONATHAN DICKINSON'S CONGREGATION IN ELIZABETHTOWN, POOLED THEIR RESOURCES, TIME, AND ENERGY, AND CONSTRUCTED *RAHWAY'S FIRST CHURCH* (IT STOOD WHERE THE MAIN DRIVEWAY ENTERS THE RAHWAY CEMETERY ON ST. GEORGES AVENUE). AT FIRST THE CONDITIONS WERE SPARTAN. ON FREEZING WINTER SUNDAYS THE FAITHFUL FOUGHT THE COLD WITH LAYERS OF CLOTHING AND BLANKETS!

THE ILLUSTRATED HISTORY OF UNION County...

by FRANK THORNE

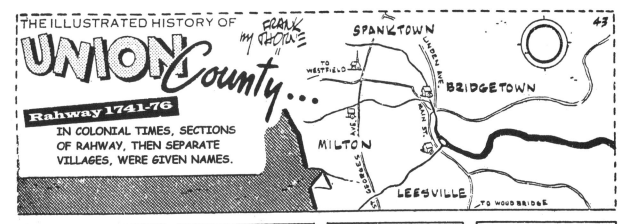

Rahway 1741-76

IN COLONIAL TIMES, SECTIONS OF RAHWAY, THEN SEPARATE VILLAGES, WERE GIVEN NAMES.

Spanktown

LEGEND TELLS US THAT THE NAME WAS DERIVED FROM AN INCIDENT WHEN A QUAKER SPANKED HIS OBSTINATE WIFE IN PUBLIC.

Milton

TRADITION HAS IT THAT THE AREA WAS NAMED FOR THE ENGLISH POET JOHN MILTON.

Leesville

THE NAME OF THIS SECTION OF LOWER RAHWAY WAS TAKEN FROM THE LEE FAMILIES IN THE AREA.

Bridge-town

IN THIS AREA, NOW THE BUSINESS DISTRICT, IS WHERE A BRIDGE SPANNED THE RAHWAY RIVER.

THE OUTBREAK OF THE WAR OF INDEPENDENCE FOUND MANY MEN FOLK RALLYING TO DISCUSS DEFENSE AND MOBILIZATION. *ABRAHAM CLARK*, A NATIVE SON OF RAHWAY, ATTENDED MANY OF THESE MEETINGS. CLARK WAS ONE OF *THE SIGNERS OF THE DECLARATION OF INDEPENDENCE* JUST A FEW MONTHS BEFORE. HE WAS VITAL IN PREPARING THE POPULACE FOR THE FIGHT.

THE ILLUSTRATED HISTORY OF
UNION County...

by FRANK THORNE

THE RAHWAY FOLK WERE EVER ALERT FOR AN ATTACK FROM THE BRITISH ON STATEN ISLAND. THEN A GROUP OF MEN RODE INTO SPANKTOWN ON OLD COUNTRY ROAD (ST. GEORGES AVENUE).

THEY STOPPED AT THE CENTER OF TOWN AND INTRODUCED THEMSELVES AS MESSENGERS OF GENERAL WASHINGTON.

THINGS WERE VERY BAD. THE AMERICAN ARMY WAS IN *FULL RETREAT* SOUTH ACROSS NEW JERSEY.

WASHINGTON WANTED TO BE SURE THE AREA WAS NOT IN THE HANDS OF THE ENEMY.

SHORTLY AFTER, ON A BITTER COLD DAY IN EARLY DECEMBER, THE PEOPLE OF RAHWAY WITNESSED THE ARRIVAL OF THE BEDRAGGLED AMERICAN ARMY. THE RESIDENTS OPENED THEIR STORAGE BARNS TO REPLENISH THE RETREATING TROOPS WITH PROVISIONS AND ARMS AS BEST THEY COULD. THEN WASHINGTON'S INEXPERIENCED FORCE CONTINUED SOUTH WITH THE REDCOATS CLOSE BEHIND!

THE ILLUSTRATED HISTORY OF UNION County...

by FRANK THORNE

THE BRITISH ARRIVED AND OCCUPIED THE TOWN, A CONTINGENT OF 500 ENEMY TROOPS REMAINED AS THE MAIN FORCE PURSUED THE RETREATING AMERICAN ARMY. THE OCCUPIERS VISITED THE HOMES OF THE TORIES.

THESE TRAITORS GUIDED THE REDCOATS IN THEIR VICIOUS RAIDS AROUND THE AREA.

THE BRITISH WOULD STEAL WHOLE STABLES OF HORSES AND DRIVE AWAY HERDS OF CATTLE.

HOUSES WERE BURNED AND AND UNARMED CITIZENS WERE CARRIED AWAY AS HOSTAGES.

AS THE OCCUPATION GROUND ON THE ATROCITIES INTENSIFIED. IT WAS AT THIS TIME THAT *EZAAK RANDOLPH* KEPT HIS TAVERN ON OLD COUNTRY ROAD AT MILTON (CORNER OF ST. GEORGES AND MILTON AVENUE). THERE WERE OTHER TAVERNS IN THE AREA, BUT THE REDCOATS FAVORED STOPPING AT 'EZAAK'S' FOR A ROUND OF YANKEE RUM. WHEN RANDOLPH AND HIS WIFE SPOTTED THE BRITISH COMING THEY WOULD HIDE IN THE WOODS, LEAVING THE ENEMY THE RUN OF THE TAVERN.

THE ILLUSTRATED HISTORY OF UNION County...

by FRANK HOWE

IN JANUARY, 1777, WASHINGTON'S REJUVENATED ARMY WON *VICTORY AFTER VICTORY!* SOON AN ORDER FROM WASHINGTON ARRIVED AT THE SHORT HILLS MILITARY CAMP.

GENERAL MAXWELL RECEIVED THE COMMAND TO DRIVE THE ENEMY FROM ALL OF CENTRAL NEW JERSEY!

HE GROUPED HIS FORCES AND THEY DROVE THE REDCOATS OUT OF NEWARK AND ELIZABETHTOWN.

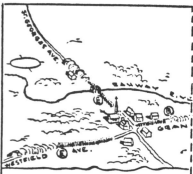

THE BRITISH RETREATED INTO SPANKTOWN (E) WHILE AN ENEMY FORCE (B) RACED FROM PERTH AMBOY TO REINFORCE THE RETREAT.

WITH THE ARRIVAL OF THE REINFORCEMENTS FROM AMBOY THE BRITISH FORCE BECAME OVERCONFIDENT AND DECIDED TO MAKE A STAND AT THE SPANKTOWN BRIDGE. THE BATTLE RAGED ON FOR TWO HOURS AND THEN THE REDCOATS MADE A HASTY RETREAT SOUTH ON WOODBRIDGE ROAD, HIGHTAILING IT BACK TO AMBOY. THE BRITISH *LOST OVER 300 MEN,* WHILE THE AMERICAN LOSSES WERE THREE KILLED AND TWELVE WOUNDED!

THE ILLUSTRATED HISTORY OF UNION County...

by FRANK HOWE

FOR FIVE MONTHS THE ENEMY MADE OCCASIONAL FORAYS INTO THE RAHWAY AREA, LOOTING AND BURNING HOMES, ONLY TO BE BEATEN BACK BY THE LOCAL MILITIA.

ON JUNE 26, 1777, NEWS REACHED RAHWAY THAT A GREAT ARMY OF 14,000 BRITISH TROOPS WAS APPROACHING!

THE ENEMY FORCE HAD PLANNED TO CRUSH WASHINGTON'S ARMY AT NEW MARKET...

...BUT THEY WERE TURNED BACK AT PLAINFIELD AND WESTFIELD. SCOUTS SOON SPOTTED THE ENEMY COLUMN APPROACHING.

THE BRITISH MADE CAMP FOR THE NIGHT. THE NEXT DAY THE AMERICAN FORCES RALLIED TO THE NORTH AND SWEPT DOWN THE RUGGED ROAD THAT IS NOW LINDEN AVENUE. THEY MADE FULL CONTACT WITH THE REDCOATS WHERE THE SECOND PRESBYTERIAN CHURCH STANDS TODAY. THE BATTLE LASTED FOR TWO HOURS, AND AGAIN THE BRITISH RETREATED. THE NEXT DAY THE ENTIRE BRITISH FORCE CROSSED OVER TO STATEN ISLAND, BRINGING PEACE TO SPANKTOWN, MILTON, LEESVILLE, AND BRIDGETOWN!

UNION County...
by FRANK "HOWE"

WITH THE END OF HOSTILITIES RAHWAY ENTERED A NEW ERA OF PROSPERITY. WITH IT THE REPUTATION OF THE *MILTON INN* GREW. IT WAS SAID THAT IT WAS THE BEST PUBLIC HOUSE IN NEW JERSEY!

EZAAK RANDOLPH, THE OWNER, HOSTED SUCH FAMOUS GUESTS AS *THOMAS JEFFERSON, JOHN ADAMS,* AND *ALEXANDER HAMILTON.*

NOW LET US IMAGINE A STAGECOACH ARRIVING AT ANOTHER FAMOUS RAHWAY INN. THE DRIVER MAKES AN ANNOUNCEMENT...

"MERCHANTS AND DROVERS, A HIGHLY RECOMMENDED PLACE FOR REFRESHMENT. WE LEAVE IN TEN MINUTES!"

WE SEE JOHN MERCEREAU'S CELEBRATED STAGECOACH THE 'FLYING MACHINE' STOPPING ON ITS WAY TO PHILADELPHIA. THE COACH LEFT HOBOKEN AT 6:30 THIS MORNING, THE TRAVELERS HAD BREAKFAST IN NEWARK AT 7:00 AND MERCHANTS AND DROVERS WAS WHERE THE PASSENGERS COULD STRETCH THEIR LEGS AND GET SOME REFRESHMENT. THE FLYING MACHINE WILL MAKE NEW BRUNSWICK BY NOON, AND BE IN PRINCETON IN TIME FOR SUPPER. THE TRAVELERS WILL ARRIVE IN PHILADELPHIA TOMORROW NOON. *THE MERCHANTS AND DROVERS TAVERN STILL STANDS AT THE CORNER OF ST, GEORGES AND WESTFIELD AVENUES. IT IS BEAUTIFULLY MAINTAINED BY THE RAHWAY HISTORICAL SOCIETY.*

THE ILLUSTRATED HISTORY OF UNION County...

by FRANK THORNE

IN 1822 REPRESENTATIVES OF SPANKTOWN, BRIDGETOWN, LEESVILLE, AND MILTON MET AND FORMALLY ADOPTED THE NAME RAHWAY, IN HONOR OF *INDIAN CHIEF RAHWACK.*

CARRIAGE MAKING SOON BECAME RAHWAY'S MOST IMPORTANT INDUSTRY.

CLOCKS OF ALL TYPES WERE MANUFACTURED HERE AND THE HARNESS INDUSTRY WAS GROWING.

PAPER MILLS, GRIST MILLS AND A FLOUR MILL WERE TURNING OUT COUNTLESS PRODUCTS FOR EXPORT.

IT WAS THE YEAR THAT *SMITH EDGAR,* THE VILLAGE PRINTER, BEGAN TO PUBLISH THE WEEKLY "BRIDGETOWN MUSEUM" FROM HIS SHOP ON MAIN STREET. WITH ALL THIS PROGRESS MUCH OF RAHWAY WAS UNDEVELOPED. THE ROADS WERE NO MORE THAN WAGON TRAILS, YET THERE WERE SHOE, CROCKERY, AND HAT STORES. RAHWAY EVEN HOSTED A FURNITURE WAREHOUSE. THE FIRST BANK WAS ESTABLISHED IN 1830.

THE ILLUSTRATED HISTORY OF UNION County...
by FRANK MOTLER

IN AUGUST, 1824, THE STATESMAN AND GENERAL *MARQUIS DE LAFAYETTE* VISITED RAHWAY. HE WAS RECEIVED WITH GREAT OVATION. LAFAYETTE WAS EN ROUTE TO WASHINGTON BY STAGE.

THE RAHWAY RIVER WAS MUCH DEEPER THEN, ALLOWING LARGE VESSELS TO SAIL UP TO DOCKS NEARER TO THE CENTER OF TOWN.

THE STEAMBOAT FROM ELIZABETHPORT TO NEW YORK LEFT AT SIX AM. TO CATCH IT FROM RAHWAY TRAVELERS HAD TO BOARD THE *BRIDGETOWN STAGE* BY FOUR. THE TRIP TOOK TWO HOURS. IN BAD WEATHER THE STAGE LEFT *CLOSER TO MIDNIGHT.*

A FAMILIAR SIGHT AROUND RAHWAY AT THAT TIME WAS OLD *THEOPHILUS PAGE* ON HIS WAY TO DELIVER SOME MAIL. MR. PAGE'S SERVICES COULD BE HAD FOR ONE CENT PER LETTER, PROVIDED THE RECIPIENT'S HOME WAS WITHIN CERTAIN BOUNDARIES. NO NEED FOR A RETURN RECEIPT, NEITHER RAIN NOR COLD NOR DARK OF NIGHT COULD KEEP OLD THEOPHILUS FROM HIS APPOINTED ROUNDS!

UNION County...

by FRANK THORNE

WHAT'S THIS? A *WAR* BREAKING OUT IN RAHWAY? NO, THE CANNON SALVOS AND CHEERING HERALD THE ARRIVAL OF THE *FIRST STEAM LOCOMOTIVE!*

IT WAS A *GREAT CELEBRATION* FOR A PROGRESSIVE TOWN THAT RECOGNIZED THE PROMISE OF THE 'IRON HORSE.'

THE ENGINE PUFFED THROUGH TOWN AT AN AMAZING *15 MILES AN HOUR!*

THE SPECTATORS HAD TO DODGE THE DANGEROUS SPARKS FROM THE BURNING OAK LOGS THAT POURED FROM THE STACK.

WHEN RAHWAY APPROACHED THE 'FASHIONABLE (EIGHTEEN) FIFTIES' IT WAS KNOWN FOR ITS CULTURAL DEVELOPMENT AND REMARKABLE VOLUME OF EXPORT ITEMS. ABOVE, ARRANGED BEHIND THE FASHIONABLE COUPLE OF THE FIFTIES, ARE TYPICAL PRODUCTS MANUFACTURED IN RAHWAY. AT THAT TIME. LEFT TO RIGHT: *CARRIAGES, SOAP, CLOTHING, CHAIRS, SHOES, CABINET FURNITURE, TINWARE, WOOLEN GOODS, HATS, CANDLES, AND CLOCKS!*

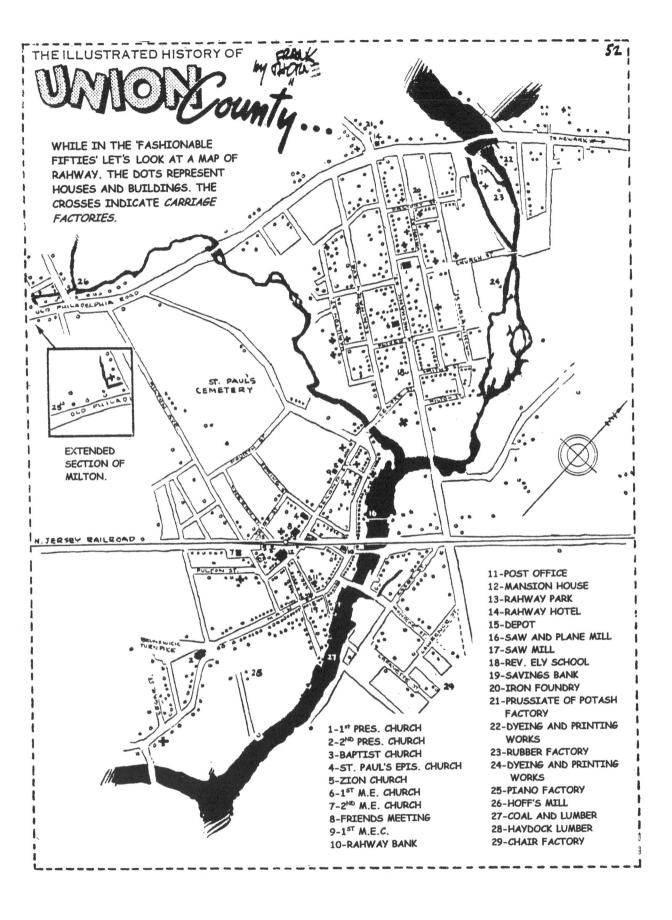

UNION County...

by FRANK

WHILE IN THE 'FASHIONABLE FIFTIES' LET'S LOOK AT A MAP OF RAHWAY. THE DOTS REPRESENT HOUSES AND BUILDINGS. THE CROSSES INDICATE *CARRIAGE FACTORIES*.

TO NEWARK

CHURCH ST.

ST. PAUL'S CEMETERY

OLD PHILADELPHIA ROAD

EXTENDED SECTION OF MILTON.

OLD PHILAD.

N. JERSEY RAILROAD

FULTON ST.

BRUNSWICK TURNPIKE

LEESNE ST.

LAWRENCE ST.

LAFAYETTE ST.

1-1ST PRES. CHURCH
2-2ND PRES. CHURCH
3-BAPTIST CHURCH
4-ST. PAUL'S EPIS. CHURCH
5-ZION CHURCH
6-1ST M.E. CHURCH
7-2ND M.E. CHURCH
8-FRIENDS MEETING
9-1ST M.E.C.
10-RAHWAY BANK

11-POST OFFICE
12-MANSION HOUSE
13-RAHWAY PARK
14-RAHWAY HOTEL
15-DEPOT
16-SAW AND PLANE MILL
17-SAW MILL
18-REV. ELY SCHOOL
19-SAVINGS BANK
20-IRON FOUNDRY
21-PRUSSIATE OF POTASH
    FACTORY
22-DYEING AND PRINTING
    WORKS
23-RUBBER FACTORY
24-DYEING AND PRINTING
    WORKS
25-PIANO FACTORY
26-HOFF'S MILL
27-COAL AND LUMBER
28-HAYDOCK LUMBER
29-CHAIR FACTORY

THE ILLUSTRATED HISTORY OF

UNION County... by FRANK THORNE

Clark

Rahway

IN 1864 THE LARGE WESTERN SECTION OF RAHWAY RECEIVED ITS CHARTER AND BECAME *CLARK TOWNSHIP*. IT WAS PRINCIPALLY FARMLAND, WITH ABOUT THREE HUNDRED INHABITANTS.

AT THIS TIME GEORGE GORDON, INVENTOR OF THE FIRST SELF-INKING PRINTING PRESS, BUILT HIS ORIGINAL FACTORY IN RAHWAY.

IN 1874 GORDON BUILT AN ELEGANT PLAYHOUSE ON IRVING STREET (ACROSS FROM PUBLIC SERVICE).

PEOPLE CAME FROM ALL OVER TO SEE PLAYS IN THE NEW THEATER. IT BECAME *THE SHOWPLACE OF NEW JERSEY!*

FOR A DECADE THE FAMOUS *GORDON OPERA HOUSE* BROUGHT ENTERTAINMENT FROM AROUND THE WORLD, MOUNTING ELABORATE PRODUCTIONS THAT DREW CROWDS FROM ALL OVER NEW JERSEY AND NEW YORK AS WELL. THEN ON THE NIGHT OF APRIL 28, 1885, *DISASTER STRUCK*. A FIRE STARTED IN FREEMAN'S CARRIAGE FACTORY NEXT DOOR. IT QUICKLY SPREAD TO THE OPERA HOUSE. FIREMEN RACED TO THE SCENE AND HAD THE BLAZE UNDER CONTROL UNTIL THE WATER MAIN BURST AND THE HOSES WERE USELESS. THE CONFLAGRATION DESTROYED THE OPERA HOUSE AND NEARLY THE ENTIRE BLOCK OF HOUSES AND STORES, ENDING RAHWAY'S SUPREMACY IN THE SUBURBAN THEATER WORLD!

THE ILLUSTRATED HISTORY OF
UNION County...

AFTER THE CIVIL WAR CARRIAGE MANUFACTURING AS RAHWAY'S PRINCIPAL INDUSTRY GAVE WAY TO THE OUTPUT OF MAJOR NEW FIRMS THAT MOVED TO TOWN.

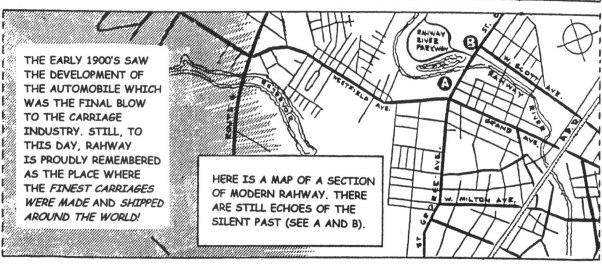

THE EARLY 1900'S SAW THE DEVELOPMENT OF THE AUTOMOBILE WHICH WAS THE FINAL BLOW TO THE *CARRIAGE* INDUSTRY. STILL, TO THIS DAY, RAHWAY IS PROUDLY REMEMBERED AS THE PLACE WHERE THE *FINEST CARRIAGES WERE MADE* AND *SHIPPED AROUND THE WORLD!*

HERE IS A MAP OF A SECTION OF MODERN RAHWAY. THERE ARE STILL ECHOES OF THE SILENT PAST (SEE A AND B).

A IN RAHWAY CEMETERY ARE THE REMAINS OF *ABRAHAM CLARK*, LAWYER, SURVEYOR, AND *SIGNER OF THE DECLARATION OF INDEPENDENCE!*

B THE MARSH HOME, 2000 ST, GEORGES AVE. BUILT IN THE EARLY 1700'S. THE MARSH FAMILY OWNED A VAST TRACT OF LAND AND WAS ESSENTIAL TO THE EARLY HISTORY OF RAHWAY. WHILE PLOWING IN A FIELD BEHIND THE HOUSE A REVOLUTIONARY CANNON WAS UNEARTHED. IT IS DISPLAYED ON THE PROPERTY TO THIS DAY.

NOTE: THE MARSH HOUSE HAS SINCE BEEN MOVED TO DIANTONIO DRIVE OFF MAURICE AVENUE.

THE ILLUSTRATED HISTORY OF UNION County...

by FRANK THORNE

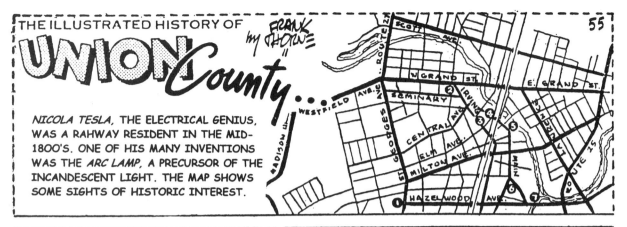

NICOLA TESLA, THE ELECTRICAL GENIUS, WAS A RAHWAY RESIDENT IN THE MID-1800'S. ONE OF HIS MANY INVENTIONS WAS THE *ARC LAMP*, A PRECURSOR OF THE INCANDESCENT LIGHT. THE MAP SHOWS SOME SIGHTS OF HISTORIC INTEREST.

① BAUMANN'S FLORIST. BETWEEN THE HOUSE AND THE STORE IS A WONDERFULLY PRESERVED PIECE OF INDIAN MORTAR.

② NEXT TO THE RAHWAY ARTS GUILD STOOD THE GORDON PRESS FACTORY.

③ THE GORDON OPERA HOUSE STOOD OPPOSITE PUBLIC SERVICE ON IRVING STREET.

④ THE *OLD MARSH* HOME AT THE FOOT OF ELM AVENUE IS SAID TO BE THE OLDEST IN RAHWAY.

⑤ ROBINSON'S HARDWARE, SITE OF THE FAMOUS *PEACE TAVERN*.

⑥ SECOND PRESBYTERIAN CHURCH, SITE OF A CRITICAL BATTLE IN THE WAR FOR INDEPENDENCE.

⑦ SOUTH BRANCH OF THE RAHWAY RIVER LOCATION OF THE FIRST MILL IN RAHWAY.

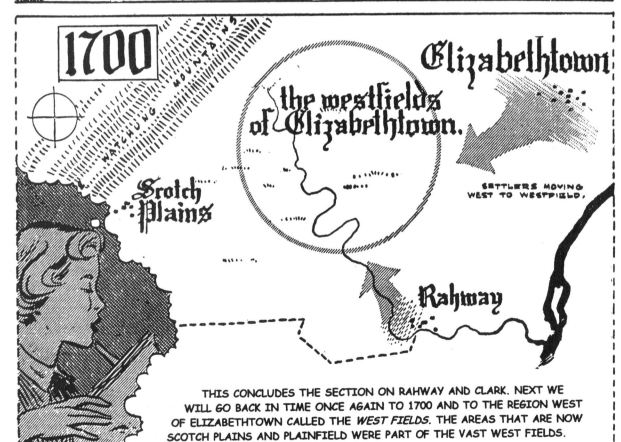

THIS CONCLUDES THE SECTION ON RAHWAY AND CLARK. NEXT WE WILL GO BACK IN TIME ONCE AGAIN TO 1700 AND TO THE REGION WEST OF ELIZABETHTOWN CALLED THE *WEST FIELDS*. THE AREAS THAT ARE NOW SCOTCH PLAINS AND PLAINFIELD WERE PART OF THE VAST WEST FIELDS.

NOTE: BAUMANN'S FLORIST SHOP AND THE MARSH HOME ON ELM HAVE SINCE BEEN RAZED.

THE ILLUSTRATED HISTORY OF UNION County...

by FRANK HOWE

WE PAUSE AND CONSIDER THE GREAT TRACT OF LAND TO THE WEST OF ELIZABETHTOWN (A ON MAP). IT WAS KNOWN AS *THE WEST FIELDS.* THE FERTILE AREA ATTRACTED MANY STALWART PIONEERS.

ELIZABETHTOWN

RAHWAY

THEY ARRIVED AS EARLY AS 1676. THE SETTLEMENTS OF THE WEST FIELDS GREW STEADILY, DEVELOPING AS A PART OF ELIZABETHTOWN.

IN 1685 A NUMBER OF *QUAKER* FAMILIES FROM RAHWAY SETTLED IN THE WEST FIELDS.

SLAVEHOLDING FAMILIES WERE COMMON TO THE AREA OF UNION COUNTY IN COLONIAL TIMES. *INDIANS* WERE KEPT IN SERVITUDE AS WELL.

SLAVERY WAS *GENERALLY PRACTICED* THROUGHOUT THE AMERICAN COLONIES. THE FIRST SLAVES WERE BROUGHT TO THE FIRST ENGLISH SETTLEMENT IN *JAMESTOWN, VIRGINIA, IN 1619.* BUT EARLY ON THERE WAS OPPOSITION TO THE PRACTICE. THE FIRST ORGANIZED CHALLENGE CAME FROM THE *QUAKER COMMUNITY* WHO MADE THEIR FIRST STATEMENT AGAINST THE CUSTOM IN 1724.

THE ILLUSTRATED HISTORY OF
UNION County...

by FRANK THORNE

AFTER JULY 4, 1776, WESTFIELD WAS ESTABLISHED AS A MILITARY POST. AS WINTER DREW NEAR, THINGS LOOKED BLEAK FOR THE RETREATING AMERICAN ARMY. THEN THE EVACUATION BEGAN.

DRIVING HERDS OF CATTLE, CROWDS OF REFUGEES MOVED SLOWLY THROUGH TOWN WITH THEIR WORLDLY POSSESSIONS PILED IN CARTS AND WAGONS. THEY SOUGHT SHELTER IN THE WATCHUNG MOUNTAINS FOR THEY KNEW THE BRITISH ARMY WOULD SOON ARRIVE AT ELIZABETHTOWN AND BEGIN THEIR OCCUPATION. THE HEARTRENDING EXODUS BROUGHT THE REALITY OF WAR TO WESTFIELD.

DURING THE FRIGID DECEMBER OF '76 THERE WERE LARGE STATIONS OF REDCOATS BILLETED AT SPANKTOWN AND ELIZABETHTOWN. WITH THE ENEMY SO CLOSE, SCOUTS, LOCAL MEN WHO KNEW THE LAY OF THE LAND, WOULD KEEP AN EYE ON THE REDCOATS AND REPORT ANY TROOP MOVEMENTS TO GENERAL MAXWELL OF THE AMERICAN COMMAND. THERE WERE MANY OF THESE BRAVE MEN, BUT ONE, *ROBERT FRENCH*, WHO LIVED NEAR THE SOUTH SPRINGFIELD ROAD (BEYOND ECHO LAKE), WAS OUTSTANDING IN HIS SHREWD WAYS OF AVOIDING CAPTURE BY THE ENEMY. ROBERT'S WIFE, *RACHAEL*, WAS JUST AS CUNNING IN MATTERS OF CAPTURE, AND A TRUE HEROINE OF THE TIME, AS WE SHALL SEE!

THE ILLUSTRATED HISTORY OF
UNION County...
by FRANK HOWE

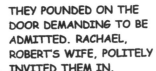

ROBERT FRENCH HAD EFFECTIVELY CARRIED OUT MANY SCOUTING MISSIONS FOR THE CONTINENTAL ARMY. THE BRITISH PUT A PRICE ON HIS HEAD. "WE MUST CAPTURE THIS MAN!" SNAPPED A BRITISH OFFICER TO HIS SUBORDINATES.

IN EARLY DECEMBER A SAVVY GROUP OF REDCOATS FOUND THE LOCATION OF THE FRENCH FARM.

THEY POUNDED ON THE DOOR DEMANDING TO BE ADMITTED. RACHAEL, ROBERT'S WIFE, POLITELY INVITED THEM IN.

FORTUNATELY, ROBERT HAD SEEN THEIR APPROACH AND HID IN THE BARN BEHIND THE HOUSE.

"MY HUSBAND HAS GONE TO THE MILL WITH SOME FRIENDS," WAS THE ANSWER RACHAEL GAVE TO THE QUESTIONING ABOUT ROBERT. "STRANGE THAT ALL THE MEN IN THE COMMUNITY HAVE GONE TO THE MILL," BARKED ONE OF THE TROOPERS. RACHAEL THEN OFFERED THEM SOME FOOD, WHICH THEY GOBBLED DOWN. THEY THANKED HER FOR THE MEAL AND TOOK THEIR LEAVE, BUT PLANNED TO RETURN THE NEXT EVENING AND CATCH FRENCH BY SURPRISE.

THE STEALTHY BRITISH PATROL BURST UPON THE FRENCH HOMESTEAD WELL AFTER NIGHTFALL. AGAIN, RACHAEL POLITELY ANNOUNCED THAT HER HUSBAND HAD GONE TO THE MILL.

IN TRUTH HER WARY SPOUSE ANTICIPATED THE VISIT AND HAD TAKEN COVER IN THE BARN WITH SOME FRIENDS.

AGAIN, THE REDCOATS DOUBTED HER STORY. ONE SUGGESTED THEY INSPECT THE GROUNDS AND BARN.

RACHAEL INSISTED THEY ENJOY SOME MORE OF HER DELICIOUS FOOD BEFORE THE OUTDOOR SEARCH.

AGAIN THE GLUTTONOUS REDCOATS EAGERLY ACCEPTED RACHAEL'S OFFER. THEY WERE A LOUD AND BOISTEROUS LOT, AND NOT *TOO BRIGHT* AS WE SHALL SEE. OUTSIDE, UNARMED, ROBERT AND HIS FRIENDS LEFT THEIR HIDING PLACE AND LOOKED ON HELPLESSLY FROM THE DARKNESS. THEY COULD SEE THAT RACHAEL WAS NOT IN DANGER SO THEY WAITED, HOPING FOR A FAVORABLE MOMENT TO INTERVENE. AND AS SURE AS RACHAEL'S FOOD WAS TASTY, THAT MOMENT WAS SOON TO COME!

THE ILLUSTRATED HISTORY OF
UNION County...
by FRANK HOWE

RACHAEL FRENCH COOLEY FINISHED SERVING THE BOORISH GROUP OF REDCOATS, THEN SHE SUGGESTED THEY ENJOY A ROUND OF METHEGLIN. "HONEY WATER?" GROWLED ONE OAF, "WE WANT CIDER INSTEAD!"

"HELP YOURSELVES, KIND SIRS," SHE CHIRPED. "THERE'S FRESH CIDER IN THE CELLAR, YOU CAN HAVE THE WHOLE BARREL IF YOU'D LIKE!"

THE BUMBLING LOT OF THEM MADE FOR THE CELLAR DOOR AND CLAMBERED DOWN THE STAIRS, *LEAVING THEIR MUSKETS BEHIND!*

WHILE THE MISCREANTS WERE SLOPPING DOWN THE CIDER RACHAEL *SLAMMED AND BOLTED THE DOOR!*

RACHAEL RAN TO THE DOOR AND SHOUTED FOR ROBERT AND HIS FRIENDS TO COME AT ONCE. "A SORRY LOT OF HOODLUMS THEY ARE," REMARKED ROBERT AS THE HUMILIATED REDCOATS WERE LED AWAY AS *PRISONERS OF WAR.* "NOT THE BRIGHTEST AMONG THE KING'S REGIMENTS," RACHAEL NOTED. NEWS OF RACHAEL'S ACT OF BRAVERY SPREAD THROUGHOUT THE COLONIES, WHILE ROBERT CONTINUED TO REPORT TO GENERAL MAXWELL DETAILED MOVEMENTS OF THE BRITISH FORCES.

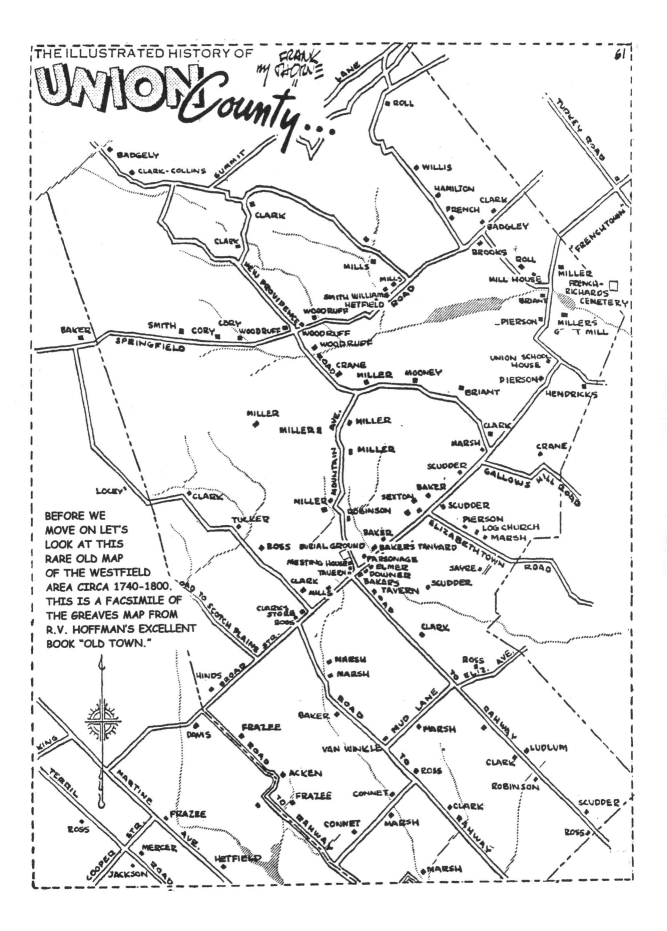

UNION County...

"my FRANK show"

BEFORE WE
MOVE ON LET'S
LOOK AT THIS
RARE OLD MAP
OF THE WESTFIELD
AREA CIRCA 1740-1800.
THIS IS A FACSIMILE OF
THE GREAVES MAP FROM
R.V. HOFFMAN'S EXCELLENT
BOOK "OLD TOWN."

THE ILLUSTRATED HISTORY OF UNION County...

by FRANK THORNE

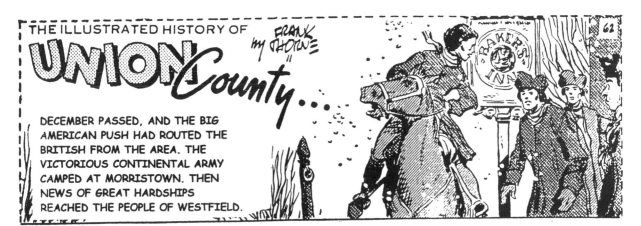

DECEMBER PASSED, AND THE BIG AMERICAN PUSH HAD ROUTED THE BRITISH FROM THE AREA. THE VICTORIOUS CONTINENTAL ARMY CAMPED AT MORRISTOWN. THEN NEWS OF GREAT HARDSHIPS REACHED THE PEOPLE OF WESTFIELD.

"IT'S SO BITTERLY COLD, A PITIFUL SIGHT," REPORTED ONE MAN WHO HAD BEEN TO THE ENCAMPMENT.

"TROOPS WITHOUT ADEQUATE CLOTHING, THEIR FEET WRAPPED IN BURLAP. FROSTBITE, DISEASE, MANY ARE DYING!"

THE WOMEN OF THE AREA BEGAN MAKING CLOTHING OF ALL TYPES TO SEND TO THE SUFFERING TROOPS.

FINALLY SPRING ARRIVED, AND IN THE WELCOME WARMTH OF MAY GENERAL WASHINGTON MOVED HIS ARMY SOUTH TO MIDDLEBROOK. LATER IN JUNE OF 1777 A CONFERENCE IN PERTH AMBOY SETS THE SCENE FOR ONE OF THE MOST CHERISHED INCIDENTS OF THAT PERIOD. *GENERAL HOWE* AND *GENERAL CORNWALLIS* WERE AT THE BRITISH HEADQUARTERS DEVISING A PLAN TO DRAW WASHINGTON'S TROOPS DOWN FROM HIS MIDDLEBROOK MOUNTAIN STRONGHOLD SO THEY COULD ONCE AND FOR ALL CRUSH THE REBEL ARMY. THEIR PLAN WAS TO FOOL WASHINGTON INTO THINKING THE REDCOATS WERE ABOUT TO MOVE ON PHILADELPHIA. HEARING THE RUMOR, GENERAL WASHINGTON MOVED HIS FORCES TO NEW MARKET. THE BRITISH IMMEDIATELY STRUCK OUT FOR NEW MARKET 14,000 STRONG!

THE ILLUSTRATED HISTORY OF UNION County...

by FRANK THORNE

AT THE BEND OF RARITAN ROAD IN SCOTCH PLAINS, WHERE TERRILL ROAD BEGINS, STILL STANDS THE HOME OF AUNT BETTY FRAZEE. ON THAT SULTRY AFTERNOON ON JUNE 26, 1777, AUNT BETTY WAS AT HOME BAKING BREAD FOR THE CONTINENTAL ARMY.

LITTLE DID SHE KNOW THAT THE BRITISH ARMY HAD LEFT AMBOY IN THE MORNING, HEADED FOR NEW MARKET.

THE ENEMY FORCE HAD BEEN TURNED BACK AT NEW MARKET, AND WERE IN TACTICAL RETREAT.

LATER, THE SOUNDS OF CANNON FIRE ROCKED THE COUNTRYSIDE.

AUNT BETTY'S LOAVES WERE BROWNING NICELY. A DELICIOUS ODOR WAFTED FROM THE STEAMING OVEN. THEN THE SOUND OF HOOFBEATS CAME FROM THE DIRT ROAD NEARBY. "THE SOLDIERS MUST BE COMING FOR THE BREAD," SHE MUSED. THE CONTINENTALS USUALLY CAME AROUND NIGHTFALL, SO SHE WENT TO THE SIDE OF THE HOUSE TO BETTER GREET THE APPROACHING HORSEMEN. "REDCOATS," SHE GASPED, BUT THEN SHE NOTICED SOMETHING DIFFERENT ABOUT THEM.

UNION County...

AUNT BETTY FRAZEE STOOD MOTIONLESS AS THE PAIR OF REDCOATS DISMOUNTED AND APPROACHED. AS THEY DREW NEAR SHE REALIZED THEY WERE OFFICERS OF HIGH RANK!

"MADAME," SPOKE ONE, "CORNWALLIS IS THE NAME. MY FRIEND WILLIAM HOWE AND I HAVE A REQUEST."

"WE CAUGHT THE ODOR OF YOUR BAKING BREAD AND ARE TEMPTED TO ASK FOR SOME LOAVES; A RARE DELICACY FOR OUR MEN."

TREMBLING, SHE OFFERED A LOAF AND SAID "I GIVE YOU THIS IN *FEAR,* NOT IN LOVE."

GENERAL CORNWALLIS STUDIOUSLY WITHDREW HIS HAND. "THEN, MADAM, NEITHER I NOR A SOLDIER OF MINE WILL PARTAKE OF IT." THE GENERALS THEN MOUNTED AND RODE OFF. LATER AUNT BETTY WATCHED IN AWE AS THE GREAT COLUMNS OF BRITISH TROOPS FILED BY IN THE SCORCHING HEAT, PLODDING ALONG RARITAN ROAD IN THE DIRECTION OF WESTFIELD.

THE ILLUSTRATED HISTORY OF

UNION County...

by FRANK HOWE

65

THE BRITISH COLUMN PAUSED IN THE VACATED VILLAGE OF WESTFIELD. THE REDCOATS' NEW STRATEGY WAS TO SLIP THROUGH ONE OF THE MOUNTAIN PASSES AND ATTACK NEW MARKET FROM HIGH GROUND.

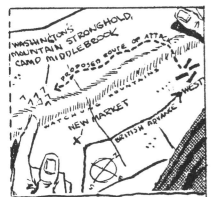

THE MOVE MUST BE SWIFT, FOR WASHINGTON WOULD SURELY RETURN TO HIS MOUNTAIN STRONGHOLD.

SCOUTS WERE SENT TO RECONNOITER AMERICAN DEFENSES AT THE MOUNTAIN PASSES TO THE WEST.

AT EVERY PASS THE SCOUTS SAW LARGE GROUPS OF WELL ARMED AMERICANS WAITING FOR JUST SUCH AN ADVANCE.

THE SCOUTS REPORTED BACK TO CORNWALLIS. HE DID NOT GLADLY RECEIVE THE NEWS. THE BRITISH GENERAL ORDERED CAMP TO BE MADE FOR THE NIGHT. THE NEXT AFTERNOON HIS ARMY QUIT WESTFIELD, MARCHED THROUGH RAHWAY, AND FERRIED BACK TO STATEN ISLAND. HAD THE ENEMY FORCE BEEN ABLE TO PENETRATE THE WATCHUNGS AND ATTACKED THE CONTINENTAL ARMY FROM THE REAR THE ENTIRE COURSE OF THE WAR FOR INDEPENDENCE MIGHT HAVE CHANGED!

THE ILLUSTRATED HISTORY OF UNION County...

Westfield

A MILITARY POST WAS ESTABLISHED IN WESTFIELD EARLY IN THE CONFLICT. THE DARING *MAD ANTHONY WAYNE* AND HIS BRIGADE WERE STATIONED HERE IN 1779.

THIS MAP OF WESTFIELD FROM THE PERIOD SHOWS: (A) THE ARSENAL AND THE DRILL GROUNDS. (B) BAKER'S INN. (C) MEETING HOUSE. (D) THE HOME OF ROBERT FRENCH.

FOR THREE YEARS THINGS WERE QUIET IN THE VILLAGE. THEN, ON JUNE 23, 1780, THE SOUND OF CANNON-FIRE ECHOED THROUGH THE LITTLE FARMING COMMUNITY.

A FIERCE BATTLE WAS RAGING IN NEARBY SPRINGFIELD BETWEEN THE BRITISH AND THE LOCAL MILITIA. THE REDCOATS, UPON HEARING THAT THE CONTINENTAL ARMY, UNDER GENERAL WASHINGTON, WAS LEAVING THE MORRISTOWN ENCAMPMENT TO JOIN THE FIGHT, RETREATED THROUGH VARIOUS ROUTES. ONE FORAGING GROUP APPROACHED WESTFIELD. YOUNG MRS. PIERSON, WHO LIVED NEAR THE ARSENAL, SPOTTED THEM FIRST. SHE TURNED AND SHOUTED "THE REDCOATS ARE COMING!"

THE ILLUSTRATED HISTORY OF
UNION County...
by FRANK THORNE

Westfield

THE BRITISH TROOPS APPROACHED THE PIERSON HOME. THE OFFICER IN CHARGE COLDLY SUGGESTED THEY WOULD NOT BE HARMED IF THEY GAVE HIM THEIR STOCK OF CIDER.

MEANWHILE, CAPTAIN LITTELL AND CAPTAIN WILLIAM CLARK WITH THEIR MINUTEMEN HAD BEEN SHADOWING THE FORAGING GROUP AND LAY IN AMBUSH NEARBY.

THE REDCOATS GREW MORE DEMANDING AND INSULTING. THEN, AS THE MINUTEMEN WATCHED MRS. PIERSON WAS FORCED TO THE WALL AT THE POINT OF A BAYONET!

CAPTAIN LITTELL, A SKILLED SHARPSHOOTER, RAISED HIS FLINTLOCK, TOOK CAREFUL AIM, PULLED THE TRIGGER, AND FIRED!

THE ILLUSTRATED HISTORY OF UNION County...
by FRANK THORNE

Westfield

CAPTAIN LITTELL'S EXPERT SHOT WOUNDED THE SOLDIER THAT WAS THREATENING MRS. PIERSON. THE UNEXPECTED VOLLEY THREW THE REDCOATS INTO DISARRAY, AND THEY BEGAN AN IMMEDIATE WITHDRAWAL.

IN THEIR HASTY RETREAT ONE OF THEIR CANNONS SWUNG AGAINST A ROCK AND THE RIGHT PIVOT, OR 'HORN,' WAS BROKEN OFF.

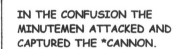

IN THE CONFUSION THE MINUTEMEN ATTACKED AND CAPTURED THE *CANNON.

LITTELL HELD HIS POSITION AS THE BRITISH FELL BACK ALONG BROAD STREET.

*THE CANNON, KNOWN AS 'OLD ONE HORN,' IS ON DISPLAY IN FAIRVIEW CEMETERY.

THE ILLUSTRATED HISTORY OF UNION County...

by FRANK FROLE

Westfield

THE ENEMY TROOPS HALTED AT OLD FIRST CHURCH. THE BELL HAD BEEN TOLLING INCESSANTLY SINCE THE INCIDENT AT THE PIERSON FARM.

THE TOLLING BELL WAS MEANT TO SUMMON THE MINUTEMEN TO ACTION!

THE CLANGING IRRITATED THE BRITISH COMMANDER. HE KNEW IT WAS SOUNDING AN ALARM.

HE ORDERED THE BELL BE REMOVED FROM THE BELFRY AND CARTED AWAY!

THE REDCOATS THEN STIFFLY MARCHED FROM THE VILLAGE TAKING THE BELL WITH THEM. THEY MARCHED EAST AND CROSSED THE KILL BACK TO STATEN ISLAND. THE OCCURRENCE WAS THE LAST MILITARY ACTION OF THIS TYPE IN THE WESTFIELD AREA. TRADITION HAS IT THAT A WESTFIELD MAN, WHO WAS IN THE SUGAR HOUSE PRISON IN MANHATTAN, HEARD THE FAMILIAR SOUND OF THE BELL IN THE DISTANCE. AT THE END OF THE WAR HE REPORTED HIS DISCOVERY AND THE BELL WAS JOYFULLY RETURNED TO THE BELL TOWER OF OLD FIRST CHURCH.

THE ILLUSTRATED HISTORY OF UNION County...
by FRANK HOLME

LIKE THE HEADLESS HORSEMAN, *THE LEGEND OF BALTUS ROLL* LINGERS IN WHAT WAS A TINY HILLTOP VILLAGE THAT LOOKED DOWN ON WESTFIELD.

BALTUS, AN EASY-GOING FARMER AND TRADER, RETIRED EARLY ON THAT COLD FEBRUARY NIGHT IN 1831. HE AND HIS WIFE LIVED A QUIET, SECLUDED LIFE.

HE WAS BY NO MEANS A RICH OR FAMOUS MAN, BUT UNKNOWN TO HIM, SOON HIS NAME WOULD BECOME FAMILIAR ON *TWO CONTINENTS*. HE AND HIS SPOUSE SLEPT THE SLEEP OF THE INNOCENT.

AROUND MIDNIGHT MRS. ROLL WAS AWAKENED BY A POUNDING ON THE ENTRANCE. SHE REFUSED TO OPEN THE DOOR. SUDDENLY THE DOOR BURST OPEN AND TWO STRANGERS ENTERED. THE MEN SEIZED ROLL FROM HIS BED, BEAT HIM, AND DRAGGED HIM OUT INTO THE SNOWY DARKNESS.

THE ILLUSTRATED HISTORY OF

UNION County... by FRANK HOWE

ORDERING BALTUS' WIFE TO STAY IN THE HOUSE, THE SCOUNDRELS HAULED HER DAZED HUSBAND INTO THE NIGHT. SHE COULD HEAR HIM CALLING FOR HER AND HIS HEARTRENDING PLEAS FOR MERCY.

IGNORING THE WARNING, ROLL'S WIFE WENT OUT THE DOOR AND TRACKED THE CULPRITS IN THE DEEP SNOW.

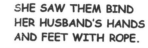
SHE SAW THEM BIND HER HUSBAND'S HANDS AND FEET WITH ROPE.

THEN TO HER HORROR THEY THREW ROLL INTO A POOL OF ICY WATER! SHE NO LONGER HEARD HIS CRIES FOR HELP.

DISTRAUGHT, SHE SLIPPED AWAY; WANDERING AIMLESSLY THROUGH A FREEZING RAIN.

TIME PASSED, AND SHE RETURNED TO THE SCENE AND FOUND BALTUS' LIFELESS BODY IN A SNOW BANK.

FEARING THE KILLERS MIGHT BE IN HER HOUSE, SHE STUMBLED TOWARD A NEARBY HOME.

THE ILLUSTRATED HISTORY OF
UNION County...
by FRANK THORNE

IN THE HOME OF JESSE CAHOON, MRS. ROLL TEARFULLY RELATED WHAT HAPPENED. AT FIRST THEY THOUGHT SHE HAD LOST HER MIND, THEN THEY SUMMONED OTHER NEIGHBORS AND WENT TO THE SCENE.

THEY FOUND THAT THE TERRIBLE STORY WAS TRUE! THE NEWS SPREAD QUICKLY IN AMERICA AND THE CONTINENT OVER THE NEW UNDERSEA LINKS WITH EUROPE. IT WAS CALLED 'THE CRIME OF THE CENTURY!'

SUSPICION AT ONCE SETTLED ON TWO SHIFTLESS HOOLIGANS: PETER B. DAVIS AND LYCIDIAS BALDWIN. THE APPARENT MOTIVE WAS ROBBERY, FOR IT WAS RUMORED THAT BALTUS HID SUMS OF MONEY IN HIS HOUSE.

DAVIS WAS APPREHENDED FIRST, AND WHEN BALDWIN HEARD OF IT HE FLED TO MORRIS-TOWN AND COMMITTED SUICIDE. DAVIS WAS ACQUITTED ON THE MURDER CHARGE, BUT JAILED FOR 24 YEARS FOR OTHER CRIMES.

SOME SAY ON MOONLIT WINTER NIGHTS THE GHOST OF OLD BALTUS CAN BE SEEN STALKING THE COUNTRYSIDE!

THE ILLUSTRATED HISTORY OF UNION County...
by FRANK THORNE

WESTFIELD WAS A FARMING AREA FROM THE BEGINNING BUT BY THE EARLY 1800'S OTHER COMMODITIES WERE PRODUCED, AMONG THEM WERE PAPER, FLOUR AND GRAIN, CIDER, AND TANNING GOODS.

IN 1818 THE FIRST SCHOOL OPENED AT THE BADGLEY HOME ON THE MOUNTAIN TOP.

AT THAT TIME THE 'SPEEDWELL STAGE' MADE REGULAR TRIPS TO ELIZABETHTOWN POINT.

IN 1838 THE ELIZABETH-TOWN AND SOMERVILLE RAILROAD BEGAN ROLLING THROUGH WESTFIELD.

Westfield
1847 ~ PLAINFIELD
1870 ~ CRANFORD
1877 ~ SCOTCH PLAINS
1877 ~ FANWOOD
1895 ~ MOUNTAINSIDE

THE WEST FIELDS, AS WE HAVE SEEN, ENCOMPASSED A VAST AREA; BUT AS THE YEARS WENT ON VILLAGES THAT WERE PART OF THE REGION SEPARATED AND BECAME INDIVIDUAL TOWNS. WESTFIELD HAD DIMINISHED IN SIZE, BUT WESTFIELD IS JUSTLY PROUD OF ITS OFF-SPRINGS!

THE ILLUSTRATED HISTORY OF UNION County...

by FRANK THORNE

TODAY, WESTFIELD IS ONE OF THE COUNTY'S MOST PROGRESSIVE TOWNS. SINCE ITS FORMATION IN 1794, THE MUNICIPALITY HAS UNDERGONE MANY CHANGES.

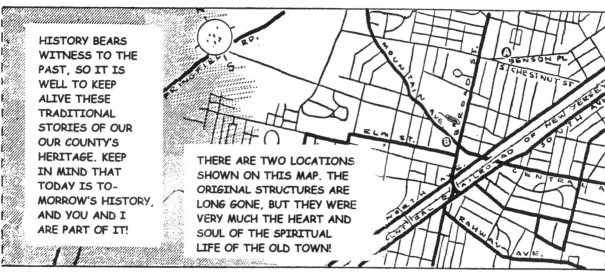

HISTORY BEARS WITNESS TO THE PAST, SO IT IS WELL TO KEEP ALIVE THESE TRADITIONAL STORIES OF OUR OUR COUNTY'S HERITAGE. KEEP IN MIND THAT TODAY IS TO-MORROW'S HISTORY, AND YOU AND I ARE PART OF IT!

THERE ARE TWO LOCATIONS SHOWN ON THIS MAP. THE ORIGINAL STRUCTURES ARE LONG GONE, BUT THEY WERE VERY MUCH THE HEART AND SOUL OF THE SPIRITUAL LIFE OF THE OLD TOWN!

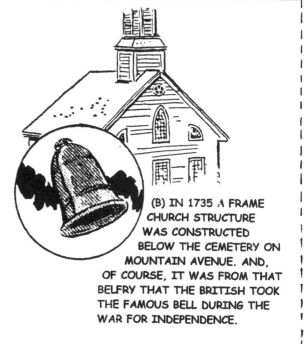

(A) *BENSON PLACE*, ONCE CALLED ELIZABETHTOWN ROAD, WAS WHERE THE EARLY SETTLERS CONSTRUCTED THE FIRST CHURCH BUILDING IN THE WEST FIELDS.

(B) IN 1735 A FRAME CHURCH STRUCTURE WAS CONSTRUCTED BELOW THE CEMETERY ON MOUNTAIN AVENUE. AND, OF COURSE, IT WAS FROM THAT BELFRY THAT THE BRITISH TOOK THE FAMOUS BELL DURING THE WAR FOR INDEPENDENCE.

UNION County...

by FRANK THORNE

WE VISITED OLD ELIZABETHTOWN, (4) ON MAP, IN THE FIRST SECTION OF THIS BOOK. THEN WE RETURNED TO THE EARLY DAYS OF RAHWAY AND CLARK, (1) AND (2), NOW WE SHALL ENTER OUR TIME MACHINE AGAIN AND DROP IN ON HISTORIC *PLAINFIELD* AND *SCOTCH PLAINS.*

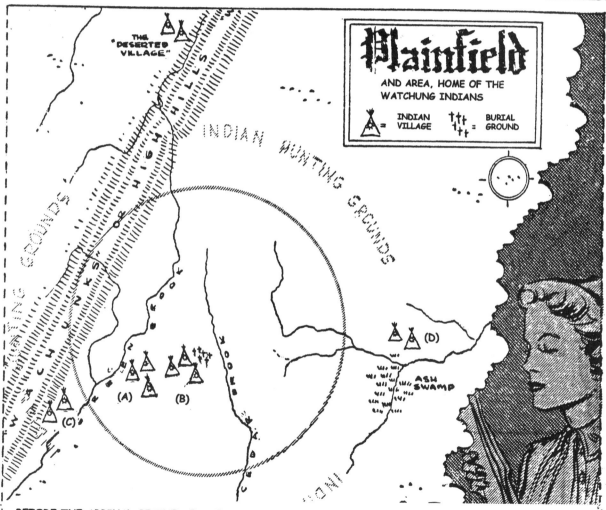

THE "DESERTED VILLAGE"

INDIAN HUNTING GROUNDS

Plainfield

AND AREA, HOME OF THE WATCHUNG INDIANS

△ = INDIAN VILLAGE   ††† = BURIAL GROUND

(A) (B) (C) (D)

ASH SWAMP

BEFORE THE ARRIVAL OF THE SETTLERS THE PLAINFIELD AREA WAS HOME TO THE WATCHUNG TRIBE OF THE DELAWARE INDIANS. THREE VILLAGES WERE LOCATED IN WHAT IS NOW CENTRAL PLAINFIELD, (A) ABOVE ON MAP, BETWEEN CLINTON AND GRANT AVENUES. (B) AN ANCIENT INDIAN BURIAL GROUND ADJOINED THE VILLAGE NEAR PARK AND EIGHTH STREET. THE THIRD VILLAGE, (C), STOOD ON GREEN BROOK NEAR WHERE SEABRING'S MILL WAS CONSTRUCTED IN COLONIAL TIMES. (D) ON MAP INDICATES ANOTHER INDIAN SETTLEMENT IN THE WILLOW GROVE AREA OF SCOTCH PLAINS. THE VILLAGES WERE SITUATED OFF WHAT IS NOW RARITAN ROAD AND LAKE AVENUE. THERE WAS A SIZABLE BURIAL GROUND IN THE VICINITY OF THE UNION COUNTY TECHNICAL INSTITUTE.

THE ILLUSTRATED HISTORY OF UNION County...
by FRANK HOWE

TWENTY YEARS HAD PASSED SINCE THE BEGINNING OF THE FIRST SETTLEMENT AT ELIZABETHTOWN. DURING THAT PERIOD A FEW WHITE HUNTERS HAD EXPLORED TO THE WEST THROUGH THE WILDERNESS OF THE PLAINFIELD REGION.

AT THAT TIME A BOAT FROM SCOTLAND ARRIVED AT PERTH AMBOY CARRYING THE FIRST WHITE SETTLERS OF THE PLAINFIELD AREA.

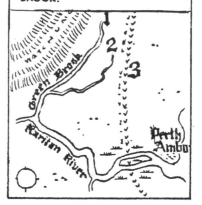

THEY TRAVELED INLAND BY BOAT UP THE RARITAN RIVER, TURNING NORTH ON GREEN BROOK.

THEY VENTURED BY LAND TO THE LEVEL LAND THAT IS NOW SCOTCH PLAINS. (1) ON MAP.

HERE THEY BEGAN THE FIRST SETTLEMENT IN THE SCOTCH PLAINS-PLAINFIELD EXPANSE. FIRST THEY BUILT THE STURDY AND CRUDE 'WICKIUPS' TO PROTECT THEM FROM THE ELEMENTS. THE LOCAL INDIANS WERE SMALL IN NUMBER AND FRIENDLY. ABOUT TWO MILES TO THE SOUTH THOMAS GORDON, ANOTHER SCOTSMAN, BUILT A WIGWAM, (2), ON WHAT BECAME THE OLD MARTINE ESTATE ON WATCHUNG AVENUE, GORDON IS CREDITED AS THE FIRST SETTLER IN PLAINFIELD. A YEAR LATER NEWS REACHED GORDON THAT A GROUP OF QUAKERS HAD MOVED FROM RAHWAY INTO WHAT IS NOW SOUTH PLAINFIELD, (3), ON MAP.

THE ILLUSTRATED HISTORY OF UNION County...
by FRANK THORNE

FOR DECADES 'THE SCOTCH PLAINS' WAS THE LARGEST SETTLEMENT WEST OF ELIZABETHTOWN, IN 1743 THE BAPTISTS FORMED THE FIRST CHURCH IN SCOTCH PLAINS. THE PLAINFIELD AREA REMAINED LARGELY UNDEVELOPED.

1700 Blondyn Plains

PLAINFIELD HAS HAD MANY NAMES. THE FIRST, "BLONDYN PLAINS," WAS FOUND ON AN OLD INDIAN DEED DATING BEFORE 1700.

1750 Blue Hills

THE FULL NAME IS "BLUE HILLS PLANTATION." TRADITION TELLS US THAT QUAKER JOHN LAING LOOKED UPON THE WATCHUNGS AND DUBBED THEM' THE BLUE HILLS.'

1775 Pinch Gut

AT THE TIME OF THE REVOLUTION THE TINY VILLAGE THAT STRETCHED ALONG GREEN BROOK WAS NARROW. IT WAS CALLED "PINCH GUT."

1790 Milltown

THE NAME MILLTOWN WAS DRAWN FROM THE NUMBER OF MILLS IN THE VILLAGE. IN 1800 THE FIRST POST OFFICE WAS ESTABLISHED WITH THE NAME "PLAINFIELD,"

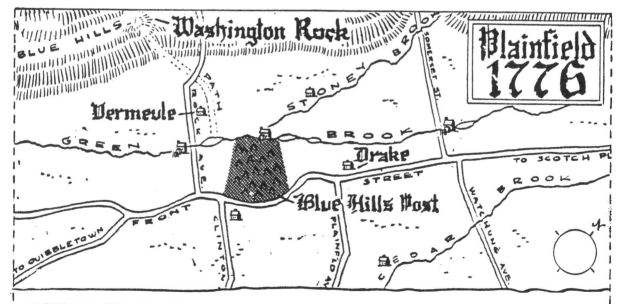

THE YEAR IS 1776 AND THE WAR FOR INDEPENDENCE IS RAGING. THE TINY BLUE HILLS PLANTATION OF 55 SOULS HAD THE REALIZATION OF THE WAR BROUGHT TO THEIR DOORSTEPS WHEN THE BLUE HILLS MILITARY POST WAS ESTABLISHED ON THE MAIN ROAD THROUGH THE COMMUNITY.

THE ILLUSTRATED HISTORY OF
UNION County...

by FRANK THORNE

WINTER DREW NEAR AT THE BLUE HILLS MILITARY POST. GENERAL WINDS MADE QUARTERS IN THE VERMEULE HOME NEARBY. THE REPORTS OF AMERICAN DEFEATS ON LONG ISLAND WORRIED THE GENERAL AND HIS MEN.

THEN NEWS OF THE RETREAT OF THE DEFEATED AMERICAN FORCES ACROSS NEW JERSEY REACHED THE BLUE HILLS POST.

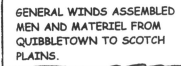

GENERAL WINDS ASSEMBLED MEN AND MATERIEL FROM QUIBBLETOWN TO SCOTCH PLAINS.

AND SO "FORT STONY BROOK" WAS ESTABLISHED WITH TWO THOUSAND TROOPS. IT WAS LESS A FORT THAN A FORTIFIED ENCAMPMENT.

THROUGH LATE WINTER AND SPRING OF '77 THERE WAS A LARGE CONCENTRATION OF BRITISH FORCES IN THE NEW BRUNSWICK AREA. INEVITABLY, THE TROOPS OF FORT STONY BROOK WERE DRAWN INTO SEVERAL SKIRMISHES WITH THE REDCOATS ON THE QUIBBLETOWN ROAD. ON SEVERAL OCCASIONS GENERAL WASHINGTON, WHO WAS HEADQUARTERED IN HIS MOUNTAIN STRONGHOLD IN THE NEARBY WATCHUNGS, USED THE VERMEULE HOUSE AS HIS COMMAND CENTER.

THE ILLUSTRATED HISTORY OF UNION County...

by FRANK THORNE

JUNE 28, 1777. IT HAD BEEN RAINING FOR SIX DAYS. IN PERTH AMBOY THE BRITISH GENERALS HOWE AND CORNWALLIS WERE PLANNING AN ATTACK ON WASHINGTON'S ARMY THE FOLLOWING MORNING.

THE PLOT WAS OVERHEARD BY AN INFORMER. HE KNEW WASHINGTON WOULD PAY WELL FOR THE INFORMATION.

HE SLIPPED OUT OF AMBOY AND GALLOPED TOWARD NEW MARKET.

WASHINGTON PAID HIM IN SILVER FOR THE INTELLIGENCE, A METHOD THAT BOUGHT MANY A BRITISH SECRET.

WASHINGTON ORDERED HIS FORCES TO TAKE THE DEFENSIVE POSITIONS PLANNED FOR SUCH AN ATTACK. THE ENEMY WAS TO MARCH AT ONE O'CLOCK THE NEXT MORNING, WHICH LEFT LITTLE TIME FOR SLEEP. WASHINGTON'S STRATEGY WAS TO DRAW THE REDCOATS TO HIS MOUNTAIN FORTRESS AND CRUSH THE ENEMY FROM HIGH GROUND.

THE ILLUSTRATED HISTORY OF
UNION County...

AT ONE A.M. JUNE 26, THE BRITISH FORCE OF 14,000 SOLDIERS AND 3,000 SAILORS MARCHED SLOWLY NORTH OUT OF AMBOY. THE NIGHT WAS CLEAR BUT THE SIX DAYS OF RAIN COMPLICATED THE HAULING OF WAGONS AND CANNONS.

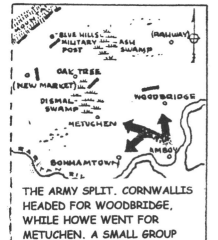

THE ARMY SPLIT. CORNWALLIS HEADED FOR WOODBRIDGE, WHILE HOWE WENT FOR METUCHEN. A SMALL GROUP MOVED SOUTH.

CORNWALLIS ENGAGED MAXWELL'S TROOPS AT WOODBRIDGE. HOWE WAS DRIVEN INTO THE SWAMP BY STIRLING'S CONTINENTALS.

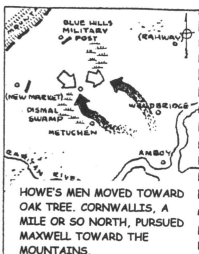

HOWE'S MEN MOVED TOWARD OAK TREE. CORNWALLIS, A MILE OR SO NORTH, PURSUED MAXWELL TOWARD THE MOUNTAINS.

AT NOON GENERAL WASHINGTON WAS RESTING IN THE *DRAKE HOUSE NEAR FORT STONY BROOK. HE HAD BEEN ON HORSEBACK ALL NIGHT INSTRUCTING HIS TROOPS ON THE STRATEGY FOR THE COMING BATTLE. WASHINGTON'S RESPITE WAS INTERRUPTED BY A MESSENGER BRINGING NEWS OF THE LATEST BRITISH ADVANCE. HE SOBERLY GATHERED HIS AIDES AND RODE UP TO WHAT IS KNOWN AS WASHINGTON ROCK TO VIEW THE COMBAT.

*THE DRAKE HOUSE STILL STANDS ON FRONT STREET IN PLAINFIELD.

THE ILLUSTRATED HISTORY OF
UNION County...
by FRANK THORNE

FROM HIS POSITION WASHINGTON WATCHED THE SLOW RETREAT OF HIS ARMY TOWARD THE MOUNTAINS. THE MOVEMENT OF GENERAL STIRLING'S GROUP HAS WASHINGTON CONCERNED.

STIRLING IS HOLDING HIS POSITION NEAR NEW MARKET, WHICH IS COUNTER TO THE PLANNED STRATEGY.

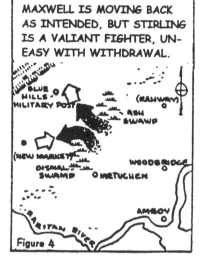

MAXWELL IS MOVING BACK AS INTENDED, BUT STIRLING IS A VALIANT FIGHTER, UNEASY WITH WITHDRAWAL.

BLUE HILLS MILITARY POST

(RAHWAY)

ASH SWAMP

(NEW MARKET)

DISMAL SWAMP

METUCHEN

WOODBRIDGE

AMBOY

RARITAN RIVER

Figure 4

FINALLY STIRLING FALLS BACK TOWARD THE MOUNTAINS, BUT HE HAD PRESSURED THE REDCOATS TO TURN NORTH.

THE BULK OF THE CONTINENTAL TROOPS WAITED IN THE MOUNTAINS AS LESS THAN THREE MILES BELOW THEM THE BRITISH PURSUED MAXWELL AND HIS MEN ALONG GREEN BROOK TOWARD THE GAP. WOULD THE REDCOATS TRY TO DRIVE THROUGH AND ATTACK WASHINGTON'S MOUNTAIN STRONGHOLD? HISTORIANS WOULD RECORD THE EVENT AS *THE BATTLE OF BLOODY GAP!*

THE ILLUSTRATED HISTORY OF UNION County...
by FRANK THORNE

THE BRITISH WERE CLOSING IN ON HOBART'S GAP. WASHINGTON HAD FEW MEN TO SPARE AS REINFORCEMENTS. HE DARED NOT RISK A WEAKENED POSITION AROUND HIS STRONGHOLD.

THE CONTINENTAL ARMY HAD MANY HOSPITALS IN THE MOUNTAINS CARING FOR TROOPS WITH INFIRMITIES.

FROM THESE HOSPITALS WAS DRAWN AN ARMY OF 3,000! THE RAGTAG BUNCH BRAVELY MARCHED TO THE GAP.

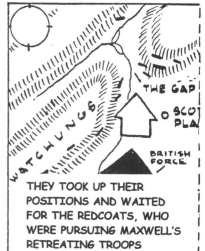

THEY TOOK UP THEIR POSITIONS AND WAITED FOR THE REDCOATS, WHO WERE PURSUING MAXWELL'S RETREATING TROOPS

THE BRITISH SWEPT INTO THE GAP, THEN MAXWELL HELD HIS GROUND AND JOINED WITH THE WAITING DEFENDERS OF THE MOUNTAIN BREACH. THE BATTLE RAGED ON, BUT SUFFERING THE WITHERING MUSKET FIRE FROM THE COMBINED AMERICAN TROOPS THE REDCOATS TURNED AND MADE A HASTY WITHDRAWAL DOWN TERRILL ROAD AND ON TOWARD WESTFIELD. *DURING THIS COMBAT, THE NEWLY SEWN AMERICAN FLAG, JUST 12 DAYS OLD, WAS FLOWN IN BATTLE FOR THE FIRST TIME!*

THE ILLUSTRATED HISTORY OF UNION County...
by FRANK HOWE

THE BRITISH ARRIVED IN WESTFIELD AND CAMPED ON THE OLD ROSS FARM, (A). AN OUTPOST OF HESSIANS BILLETED A DISTANCE AWAY AT WHAT WOULD BE AT THE SOUTH END OF GROVE STREET NEAR RAHWAY AVE, (B)

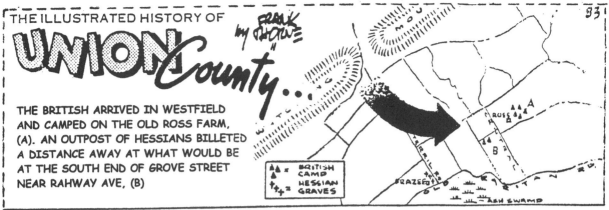

▲▲ = BRITISH CAMP
✝✝✝ = HESSIAN GRAVES

AT SUNSET COL. MORGAN PLANNED TO ATTACK THE HESSIAN ENCAMPMENT.

AFTER DARK, MORGAN'S RAIDERS FASTENED THEIR BAYONETS, AND MOVED TOWARD THE OUTPOST.

MORGAN AND HIS MEN SLAUGHTERED THE ENTIRE HESSIAN OUTPOST! THE NEXT DAY THE MAIN ENEMY ARMY WITHDREW EAST TO STATEN ISLAND.

PLAINFIELD MEETING 1788

PLAINFIELD MEETING 1727

ELEVEN YEARS LATER, ABOUT A HALF MILE EAST OF THE ABANDONED BLUE HILLS MILITARY POST, THE QUAKERS BUILT A MEETING HOUSE TO REPLACE THE ONE BUILT IN 1727 THAT STOOD ON WOODLAND AVENUE NEAR THE PLAINFIELD COUNTRY CLUB. THE PLAINFIELD QUAKER MEETING HOUSE STILL STANDS ON PARK AVENUE NEXT TO THE PLAINFIELD POST OFFICE.

THE ILLUSTRATED HISTORY OF UNION County...

by FRANK THORNE

IN THE EARLY 1800'S THE PLAINFIELD-SCOTCH PLAINS AREA, LIKE ALL OF UNION COUNTY, BEGAN TO EXPORT ITEMS OTHER THAN FARM PRODUCE. HATS, PAPER, GRAIN, AND LUMBER JOINED AN EVER LENGTHENING LIST OF MANUFACTURED GOODS.

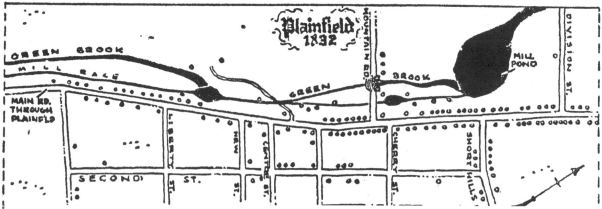

Plainfield 1832

THIS MAP OF PLAINFIELD IN 1832 SHOWS A ROBUST COMMUNITY OF 300 HOUSES, 750 INHABITANTS, 7 STORES, 8 TAILORING SHOPS, 6 HAT MANUFACTURERS, 2 WHEELSMEN, 3 BLACKSMITHS, 2 GRIST MILLS, 7 CHURCHES, AND A TOWN NEWSPAPER!

ON DECEMBER 13, 1843, *THE WASHINGTON VALLEY DEBATING SOCIETY* MET FOR THE FIRST TIME IN JOHN O. DRAKE'S STORE IN THE VALLEY. THE GROUP OFFICIALLY MET EVERY WEDNESDAY NIGHT AT 6:30. THEY DISCUSSED THE BURNING QUESTIONS OF THE DAY, SUCH AS: "WHICH SEES MOST PLEASURE, THE MARRIED OR SINGLE LIFE?" AND, "HAD WE BETTER EMIGRATE TO THE WEST OR STAY AT HOME?" DEBATE ON PUBLIC ISSUES WAS FREQUENT AND UNINHIBITED, IT IS NOT KNOWN IF ANY OF THE GOOD GENTLEMEN CAME TO BLOWS OVER CONTROVERSIAL TOPICS!

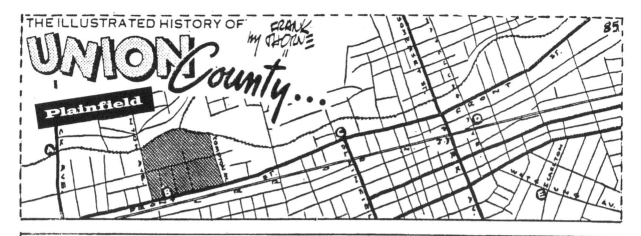

THE ILLUSTRATED HISTORY OF UNION County... by FRANK THORNE

Plainfield

(A) ROCK AVENUE AND GREEN BROOK WAS THE SITE WHERE 200 YEARS AGO CORNELIUS VERMEULE BUILT PLAINFIELD'S FIRST SAW MILL. THE SHADED AREA INDICATES THE LOCATION OF THE BLUE HILLS MILITARY POST.
(B) INDICATES LOCATION OF FORT STONY BROOK.

(C) THE DRAKE HOUSE, DATING TO 1759, IS THE CURRENT HEAD-QUARTERS OF THE PLAINFIELD HISTORICAL SOCIETY. (D) THE QUAKER MEEING HOUSE, CONSTRUCTED IN 1788. (E) THE MARTINE ESTATE, 1100 WATCHUNG AVENUE. IT WAS HERE IN 1684 THAT THOMAS GORDON BUILT A WIGWAM, AND BECAME PLAINFIELD'S FIRST WHITE SETTLER!

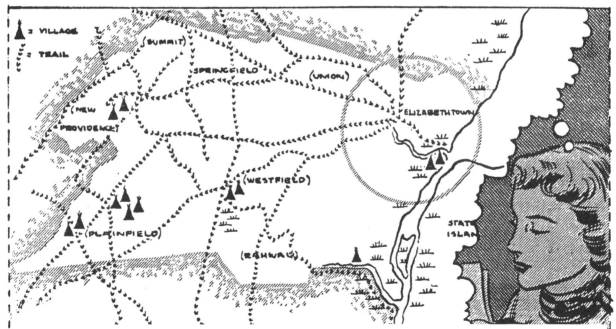

THIS ENDS THE OVERVIEW OF THE PLAINFIELD-SCOTCH PLAINS AREA OF UNION COUNTY. NOW WE SHALL RETURN TO *HISTORIC ELIZABETHTOWN* WHICH WARRANTS A MORE DETAILED LOOK AT WHAT WAS THE CRADLE OF COMMUNITY LIFE IN NEW JERSEY. THE MAP ABOVE SHOWS SOME OF THE INDIAN TRAILS THAT MADE UP THE VAST NETWORK THAT RAN THROUGH THE COUNTY BEFORE THE ARRIVAL OF THE SETTLERS. IT IS INTERESTING TO NOTE THAT MANY OF OUR MODERN ROADWAYS ROUGHLY FOLLOW THE OLD INDIAN PATHS.

THE ILLUSTRATED HISTORY OF UNION County...
by FRANK THORNE

Elizabethtown

WE WILL FINE-TUNE OUR TIME MACHINE AS WE RETURN TO HISTORIC ELIZABETHTOWN POINT. THERE WERE MANY ACCOUNTS WE MISSED THE LAST TIME WE VISITED. SO HERE WE ARE BACK IN THE YEAR 1665 ONCE AGAIN!

IT IS AUGUST AND STURDY LOG CABINS ARE BEGINNING TO REPLACE THE CRUDE INDIAN-STYLE DWELLINGS

IT WAS THE MONTH THAT THE GOOD SHIP 'PHILIP' WEIGHED ANCHOR OFF ELIZABETHTOWN POINT.

THE PIONEERS LEFT THEIR EARLY HARVESTS TO GO TO THE POINT AND WELCOME PHILIP CARTERET.

IT WAS IN ELIZABETHTOWN, THEN THE STATE CAPITAL, THAT CARTERET BEGAN HIS DRAMATIC CAREER AS THE FIRST GOVERNOR OF NEW JERSEY. WHEN CARTERET CONVENED HIS FIRST ASSEMBLY IN 1668 WITH DELEGATES FROM BERGEN, NEWARK, MIDDLETOWN, AND SHREWSBURY, IT BECAME CLEAR THAT NEW ENGLAND PURITANISM WOULD DOMINATE THE COLONY. SWEARING AND DRUNKENNESS WERE MADE PENAL OFFENSES AND THE CHILD OVER 16 WHO CURSED OR SMOTE AT HIS PARENTS MIGHT INCUR THE *DEATH PENALTY!*

THE ILLUSTRATED HISTORY OF UNION County...
Elizabethtown
by FRANK THORNE

THE SOUND OF CROWING ROOSTERS AND LOWING CATTLE REVERBERATES THROUGH THE CRISP PRE-DAWN AIR IN THE COLONY OF ELIZABETHTOWN. IT'S GOING TO BE A TYPICAL LATE SUMMER DAY AT THE POINT.

THE MAN OF THE HOUSE IS AWAKENED BY THE RUCKUS. HE SLIPS FROM UNDER HIS FEATHERBED.

HE HASTILY DRESSES AND STARTS A FIRE FROM THE SMOLDERING EMBERS OF THE PREVIOUS FIRE.

AFTER WAKING HIS KIN HE TENDS TO HIS 'CRITTERS.' EVERY PIONEER FAMILY HAD PLENTY OF LIVESTOCK.

AT THEIR SIMPLE BUT SUBSTANTIAL BREAKFAST PAPA WOULD ASSIGN THE CHORES OF THE DAY. TALK OF CURRENT EVENTS MIGHT INCLUDE THE NEW SETTLEMENT NORTH CALLED "NEW WORK," WHICH WOULD BECOME NEWARK, OR THE NEWLY ORGANIZED MILITARY COMPANY FORMED FOR THE DEFENSE OF THE VILLAGE AGAINST INDIAN ATTACK. THE LENNI LENAPES, THE LOCAL GROUP, ARE A PEACEFUL LOT, BUT THERE ARE VOLATILE TRIBES TO THE NORTH IN THE VAST AREA OF WHAT IS NOW NEW YORK STATE.

UNION County...

by FRANK THORNE

AFTER BREAKFAST THE PIONEER FARMER WOULD TACKLE THE TASKS REQUIRED OF THE SEASON. THE FARM TRACTS TYPICALLY STRETCHED FAR INTO THE WILDERNESS; THEIR BOUNDARIES WERE OFTEN IGNORED.

SETTLERS WOULD CUT THE BEST TIMBER FROM SOMEONE ELSE'S TRACT. THE WRONGED FARMERS COMPLAINED TO GOVERNOR CARTERET.

IT WAS THE TOPIC OF THE DAY WHEN THE NEWS GOT AROUND THE SETTLEMENT.

A LAW HAS BEEN PASSED PROHIBITING THE POACHING OF TREES FOR LUMBER!

OCCASIONALLY, AS THE DAY PROGRESSED, WORK MIGHT BE INTERRUPTED BY SMALL GROUPS OF LOCAL INDIANS WHO SOUGHT TO TRADE THEIR WARES. THEY OFFERED ANIMAL SKINS, CORN, AND VENISON IN RETURN FOR THE SETTLERS' GOODS. THE INDIANS ARE SELDOM SEEN, FOR THEIR VILLAGES ARE DEEP IN THE FOREST SURROUNDING THE SETTLEMENT; BUT ON FESTIVE OCCASIONS THEY COULD BE SPOTTED AT THE SHORE NEAR THE POINT GATHERING CLAM AND OYSTER SHELLS, THE RAW MATERIAL FOR WAMPUM.

THE ILLUSTRATED HISTORY OF
UNION County...
by FRANK HOWE

Elizabethtown

WHILE HER HUSBAND WAS TENDING TO HIS CROPS, THE LADY OF THE HOUSE MIGHT BE FOUND AT HER WHEEL PATIENTLY SPINNING FLAXEN THREAD.

LATER THESE STRANDS WILL BE TRANSFERRED TO HER HOMEMADE LOOM, WHERE LINEN FABRIC IS MADE.

THEN THE FABRIC IS SEWN INTO SCRATCHY OUTERWEAR AND OTHER ARTICLES OF CLOTHING.

IN APRIL AND MAY, CANDLES WERE MADE FROM TALLOW SAVED FROM LAST YEARS' BEEF AND MUTTON SUPPLY.

JUNE WAS WHEN THE WOMEN PREPARED THE SUPPLY OF *SOAP*. PRINCIPAL INGREDIENTS, LYE AND POTASH, WERE MADE BY POURING WATER THROUGH A BARREL FILLED WITH WOOD ASHES. THEN DISCARDED GREASE FROM COOKING AND BUTCHERING WAS BOILED TOGETHER IN A LARGE POT WITH THE LYE AND POTASH. THE CAKES WERE CUT FROM THE COOLED MASS. THE FEMALES OF THE VILLAGE HAD PLENTY OF OTHER JOBS TO DO: COOKING, WASHING, DRYING THE BERRY CROP OF THE SEASON, GATHERING AND DRYING HERBS... THE LIST IS EXTENSIVE. *THE WORK WAS CEASELESS; ALL YEAR LONG FROM DAWN TO WELL INTO THE NIGHTTIME HOURS.*

THE ILLUSTRATED HISTORY OF UNION County...

by FRANK THORNE

THE YEAR 1668 WAS EVENTFUL FOR THE TINY SETTLEMENT OF LESS THAN 100 FAMILIES CALLED ELIZABETHTOWN. THE FIRST GENERAL ASSEMBLY OF NEW JERSEY CONVENED IN THE VILLAGE COMMON HOUSE.

HERE THE LAWS WERE MADE. AMONG THEM A RULING THAT ANYONE FOUND AWAY FROM HIS HOME AFTER 9 PM...

THE COMMON HOUSE STOOD WHERE THE FIRST PRES-BYTERIAN CHURCH STANDS ON BROAD STREET TODAY.

...WAS QUESTIONED. IF HE COULD GIVE NO REASON FOR HIS ACTIONS HE WAS HELD AND TAKEN BEFORE THE VILLAGE MAGISTRATE.

PROMPTLY AT 9 PM THE NIGHT WATCH MADE HIS ROUNDS ON THE LOOKOUT FOR ANY VIOLATORS OF THE CURFEW, AND TO SEE THAT ALL THE LIGHTS WERE OUT. NO EXCEPTIONS WERE MADE UNLESS THERE WAS ILLNESS IN THE FAMILY. A CANDLE BURNING AFTER CURFEW WITHOUT DUE CAUSE WAS REPORTED TO THE MAGISTRATE. THE OFFENDER WOULD BE ORDERED TO APPEAR BEFORE THE MAGISTRATE TO EXPLAIN THE DISOBEDIENCE.

THE ILLUSTRATED HISTORY OF UNION County...
by FRANK THORNE

IN 1668 A GROUP OF PLANTERS GATHER ON A DIRT TRAIL, (NOW BROAD STREET) NEAR THE 'CREEK' (THE ELIZABETH RIVER), TO PROUDLY WATCH THE CONSTRUCTION OF NEW JERSEY'S FIRST MILL!

IT IS TO BE A LUMBER MILL; AND WHAT A BOON IT WILL BE IN BUILDING NEW FRAME HOUSES IN THE VILLAGE!

THE BUILDER IS JOHN OGDEN. EVERYONE KNOWS JOHN, FOR HE WAS ONE OF THE FOUNDERS OF THE SETTLEMENT.

OGDEN TELLS THE SETTLERS THAT TROUBLE IS BREWING BETWEEN THE VILLAGERS AND THE NEW GOVERNOR.

THE FARMERS ARE QUICK TO EXPRESS THEIR FEELINGS TOWARD PHILIP CARTERET. "WHEN HE CAME THREE YEARS AGO HE BROUGHT WITH HIM SOME THIRTY MEN AND WOMEN 'SERVANTS' FROM ABROAD. THEY ARE OF A DIFFERENT RELIGION AND CHARACTER. THESE LACKEYS REPRESENT EVERYTHING WE CAME HERE TO ESCAPE. AND NOW SOME OF THEM HAVE BEEN GRANTED LAND AND LIVE AMONG US!"

THE ILLUSTRATED HISTORY OF
UNION County...
Elizabethtown

THE TAVERN AT THE 'POINT' IS BUZZING WITH DISCONTENT. GOVERNOR CARTERET HAS LEVIED A TAX ON THEIR LAND THAT THEY PURCHASED FROM THE INDIANS.

"FURTHERMORE, HE CONTINUES TO GRANT LAND TO HIS 'SERVANTS' WITHOUT CONSULTING THE SETTLERS."

"HE HAS DISMISSED LUKE WATSON AS LIEUTENANT OF OUR MILITARY CORPS BECAUSE HE WAS OPPOSED TO HIS ACTIONS!"

"THE SCOUNDREL IS UNFAIRLY MEDDLING IN LOCAL AFFAIRS." FARMERS, UNCONCERNED WITH POLITICS, TOOK INTEREST.

THE SETTLERS' HOSTILITY TOWARD CARTERET BECAME MORE INFLAMED WITH EVERY PASSING DAY. "WHO GAVE THIS YOUNG STRANGER THIS KINGLY POWER? WHO SET HIM ABOVE THE REPRESENTATIVES OF THE PEOPLE? WHEN WE ASK HIM WHY HE DOES THESE THINGS HE REFUSES TO ANSWER! HE ANSWERS ONLY TO HIS MASTERS ABROAD. WE FEEL WE ARE POWERLESS. *SOMETHING MUST BE DONE!*"

THE ILLUSTRATED HISTORY OF UNION *County...*

by FRANK THORNE

THE SETTLERS' WRATH FOCUSED ON TWO OF THE GOVERNOR'S SERVANTS. RICHARD MICHEL AND HIS WIFE HAD ARRIVED WITH CARTERET SOME SIX YEARS BEFORE THE INCIDENT.

IN REWARD FOR THEIR SERVICES CARTERET HAD GRANTED THE MICHELS A PLOT OF LAND.

THE MICHELS BUILT A SMALL HOME AND FENCED IT OFF FROM THE SETTLEMENT. THE VILLAGERS BECAME FURIOUS.

AT A TOWN MEETING THEY DECIDED TO ACT. "WE WILL BE OVERRUN BY FRENCH-MEN AND FOREIGNERS!"

GRANTING LAND COULD ONLY BE DONE BY *THE PEOPLE IN PUBLIC MEETING!* IT WAS A CLEAR CASE OF *ARROGANT USURPATION OF POWER BY THE GOVERNOR.* IF THEY DID NOT RESIST CARTERET NOW THEY MIGHT AS WELL GIVE UP ALL THOUGHT OF SELF-GOVERNMENT. THE NEXT MORNING A GROUP OF DETERMINED SETTLERS GATHERED AND SET OUT FOR THE MICHEL HOME.

THE ILLUSTRATED HISTORY OF
UNION County...
by FRANK HOWE

THE ENRAGED VILLAGERS APPROACHED THE MICHEL HOME CARRYING FARM TOOLS AND STOUT CUDGELS.

RICHARD MICHEL CAME TO THE FENCE WHEN HE SAW THEIR APPROACH. HE WARNED THEM NOT TO TRESPASS ON HIS PROPERTY.

HIS PROPERTY? THAT WAS THE FINAL INSULT! THE MEN WENT INTO ACTION. MICHEL AND HIS WIFE MELTED INTO THE WOODS AND WATCHED HELPLESSLY AS THE FENCE CAME DOWN AND WAS STREWN ABOUT THE YARD. THEN SEVERAL OF THE MEN LAID WASTE TO THE GARDEN WHILE THE OTHERS ATTACKED THE HOUSE, PRYING OFF THE CLAPBOARDS AND SENDING THEM IN ALL DIRECTIONS. IT WAS WARM WORK FOR A MIDSUMMER'S DAY, BUT IT WAS A NEEDFUL ENTERPRISE. GOVERNOR CARTERET GOT THE MESSAGE.

UNION County...
by FRANK THORNE

CARTERET WAS DETERMINED TO PUNISH THE REBELS. HE ANNOUNCED THAT HE HAD CONSTITUTED A COURT TO TRY THE MEN WHO RAVAGED MICHEL'S PROPERTY.

THE COURT CONVENED IN THE TOWN HOUSE AND THE INSURGENTS WERE FOUND GUILTY OF SEDITION.

THE SO-CALLED REBELS PAID LITTLE HEED TO THE PROCEEDINGS.

THEY WERE SENTENCED TO EACH PAY A STIFF FINE, BUT THE MEN IGNORED THE ORDER OF THE COURT.

CARTERET AND HIS MINIONS WERE POWERLESS AGAINST THE WILL OF AN OUTRAGED PEOPLE! SOON AFTER THE INCIDENT CARTERET BOARDED A BOAT AND RETURNED TO ENGLAND TO GIVE A FULL REPORT OF THE REBELLION IN ELIZABETHTOWN TO HIS ROYAL SUPERIORS. PHILIP CARTERET CONSIDERED HIS DEPARTURE A TACTICAL MOVE. HE WAS DETERMINED TO RETURN AND RESUME CONTROL OF THE COLONY. WITH CARTERET GONE ELIZABETHTOWN HAPPILY RETURNED TO NORMAL.

THE ILLUSTRATED HISTORY OF

UNION County...

by FRANK HOWE

Elizabethtown

THE BREAK FROM CARTERET'S AUTOCRATIC RULE LASTED TWO YEARS. DURING THAT TIME THE SETTLEMENT GREW STEADILY.

HARVESTS WERE PLENTIFUL AND NEW HOUSES WERE BEING BUILT WITH LUMBER FROM JOHN OGDEN'S MILL.

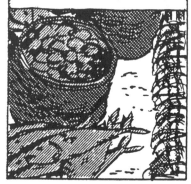

CLAMS AND OYSTERS WERE PLENTIFUL AT THE 'POINT.' INDIANS WERE OCCASIONALLY SEEN ALONG THE WATERFRONT.

YOUNGSTERS WERE WARNED AGAINST ASSOCIATING WITH THE INDIGENOUS POPULATION.

SOME CHILDREN HAD NEVER SEEN AN INDIAN. THE ELDERS WOULD TELL OF THEIR IMPRESSIONS OF THE LENNI LENAPES. "THE MALES ARE TOLERABLY STOUT, WITH A LONG LOCK OF BLACK HAIR LIKE A COCK'S COMB. THE WOMEN ARE WELL FEATURED WITH LOOSE HANGING HAIR. OVERALL THEY ARE SLOW OF SPEECH, EVEN BASHFUL. IF YOU SEE THEM BE POLITE BUT WARY AND COME INSIDE AS SOON AS POSSIBLE!"

THE ILLUSTRATED HISTORY OF
UNION County...
by FRANK THORNE

Elizabethtown

PHILIP CARTERET SAILED FROM ENGLAND AND RETURNED TO ELIZABETHTOWN DURING THE HARVEST OF 1674. HE REINSTATED HIS AUTOCRATIC RULE, BUT THIS TIME HIS EDICTS WERE EVEN MORE SEVERE. THE SETTLERS WERE VOCAL IN THEIR OPPOSITION.

"HE IS MORE CORRUPT THAN BEFORE! HE HAS STRIPPED US OF OUR RIGHTS GIVEN US IN OUR ORIGINAL GRANTS!"

"HE HAS ORDERED THAT WE HAVE OUR PROPERTY SURVEYED AGAIN, AND WE MUST PURCHASE NEW PATENTS FOR OUR LAND!"

"HE DEMANDS THE REBELS PAY THE FINES FOR THE ATTACK ON THE MICHEL HOME!"

THE PEOPLE GREW WEARY OF THESE CONFLICTS. THEY TRIED TO BARGAIN WITH THE GOVERNOR, BUT HE REMAINED ADAMANT, AND BACKED HIS STANCE WITH A SMALL COMPANY OF ARMED FLUNKIES. THE SETTLERS RELUCTANTLY ACQUIESCED, DURING THAT TIME OF RELATIVE CALM THE GOVERNOR BUSIED HIMSELF SUPERVISING THE CONSTRUCTION OF A NEW AND BIGGER HOME ON HIS PROPERTY THAT ENCOMPASSED 2,700 ACRES! CARTERET, WITH GREAT FANFARE, MOVED INTO HIS NEW RESIDENCE ALONG WITH HIS CONTINGENT OF EIGHTEEN SERVANTS.

THE ILLUSTRATED HISTORY OF

UNION County...

"by FRANK THORNE"

THE GENERAL ASSEMBLY AT ELIZABETH-TOWN HAD BEEN BUSY ADDING NEW LAWS TO THE BOOKS. IT WAS MADE UNLAWFUL TO DO ANY TYPE OF WORK, TRAVEL UNNECESSARILY OR CREATE ANY TYPE OF DISTURBANCE ON THE SABBATH.

IT HAD BEEN A PRACTICE TO LET THE ANIMALS WANDER FREELY THROUGHOUT THE SETTLEMENT.

SO STRICT NEW RULES ABOUT CONFINING LIVESTOCK TO FENCED AREAS WERE PUT IN PLACE.

LAWS REGULATING THE BRANDING OF ANIMALS WERE PASSED, AND A POUND WAS CREATED FOR STRAY LIVESTOCK.

SEVERAL TAVERNS IN THE GROWING SETTLEMENT HAD BEEN SELLING STRONG DRINK TO THE LOCAL INDIAN POPULATION, CAUSING INCIDENTS OF PUBLIC DRUNKENNESS. THE PRACTICE WAS MADE UNLAWFUL. AFTER THE SETTLERS COMPLAINED THAT INNKEEPERS WERE TOO OFTEN OVERCHARGING UNSUSPECTING TRAVELERS THE ASSEMBLY PUT A PRICE CEILING INTO EFFECT.

THE ILLUSTRATED HISTORY OF UNION County...

by FRANK HOLMES

FOURTEEN HARVESTS HAD BEEN GATHERED IN THE ELIZABETHTOWN SETTLEMENT, AND WITH EACH YEAR THE TILLED ACREAGE INCREASED. LARGE PLANTATIONS WERE ON THE RISE, WITH AN EVER-GROWING POPULATION OF COLONISTS ARRIVING.

2 ELIZABETHTOWN'S TREMENDOUS COMMERCIAL POSSIBILITIES WERE BEING REALIZED.

3 UNEXPECTEDLY, CARTERET HAD A MYSTERIOUS CHANGE OF HEART. HE SEEMED TO WANT TO BE ON GOOD TERMS WITH THE PEOPLE. THE SETTLERS VIEWED THIS NEW ATTITUDE WITH SUSPICION.

4 RIGHTLY SO, FOR SIR EDMUND ANDROS, THE NEW YORK GOVERNOR, HAD WATCHED THE RAPID GROWTH OF THE YOUNG COLONY AND INTENDED TO TAKE CONTROL OF THE AREA. CARTERET NEEDED THE PEOPLE BEHIND HIM TO HOLD ON TO HIS POLITICAL POWER BASE.

THE ILLUSTRATED HISTORY OF

UNION *County...*

Elizabethtown

"MY FRANK THORNE"

ANDROS ARROGANTLY PRESSED ON WITH HIS GREEDY PLOT, AND CLAIMED POLITICAL JURISDICTION OVER ALL OF NEW JERSEY. CARTERET REFUSED TO TURN OVER HIS POWER TO THE NEW YORK GOVERNOR.

CARTERET QUICKLY ORDERED THAT 150 ADDITIONAL MEN BE ARMED IN CASE ANDROS PLANNED TO USE FORCE.

THE TOWNSPEOPLE RALLIED BEHIND CARTERET. THEY WOULD NOT SUBMIT TO RULE FROM NEW YORK.

ABOVE ALL IT WAS SELF-RULE, BUILT ON THE DEMOCRATIC PROCESS, THAT THEY LONGED FOR.

GOVERNOR ANDROS, ACCOMPANIED BY SEVERAL OFFICERS AND COUNSEL, ARRIVED FROM NEW YORK BY BOAT. HE WENT DIRECTLY TO CARTERET'S PLANTATION MANOR HOUSE. THEY EXCHANGED SOME FORMAL COURTESIES THEN ANDROS DEMANDED, IN THE NAME OF HIS MAJESTY, THE KING OF ENGLAND, THAT CARTERET RELINQUISH HIS RULE OVER NEW JERSEY.

THE ILLUSTRATED HISTORY OF UNION County...

by FRANK THORNE

Elizabethtown

CARTERET REFUSED, ADDING THAT THE PEOPLE WERE BEHIND HIM, AND THEY WOULD NEVER SUBMIT TO RULE FROM A NEW YORK GOVERNOR.

FURTHERMORE, CARTERET WOULD OBEY ONLY BY A *DIRECT ORDER* FROM THE CROWN.

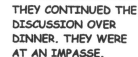

THEY CONTINUED THE DISCUSSION OVER DINNER. THEY WERE AT AN IMPASSE.

THEN ANDROS RETURNED TO HIS SHIP AND BARKED THE ORDER TO SET SAIL BACK TO NEW YORK.

SIR EDMOND ANDROS PONDERED HIS OPTIONS AS THE SHIP GLIDED ACROSS THE LOWER BAY. HE WOULD PRESS THE ISSUE AND SEND BOAT AFTER BOAT OF ARMED CONTINGENTS OF LOYALISTS TO ELIZABETHTOWN TO DEMAND SUBMISSION. THEY WOULD BE MET BY JEERING CROWDS, READY TO SHED THEIR BLOOD TO UPHOLD THEIR OWN GOVERNOR. ANDROS BACKED OFF, AND AS SPRING CAME HE HATCHED A SINISTER PLAN.

THE ILLUSTRATED HISTORY OF UNION County...

by FRANK THORNE

ANDROS ORDERED A GROUP OF HIS SOLDIERS TO SAIL TO ELIZABETHTOWN UNDER THE COVER OF DARKNESS. THEIR MISSION WAS TO KIDNAP CARTERET.

THE HEAVILY ARMED THUGS ARRIVED AT THE POINT AND DISEMBARKED.

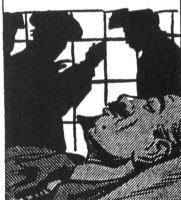

IT WAS MIDNIGHT WHEN THEY REACHED CARTERET'S HOME. HE WAS ASLEEP.

THEY DRAGGED HIM OUTSIDE. CARTERET RESISTED AND THEY BRUTALLY BEAT HIM.

THEY CARRIED CARTERET'S LIMP BODY TO THE WATERFRONT AND CAST OFF IN THE FRIGID WATERS OF THE KILL TOWARD MANHATTAN ISLAND. LATER, AS CARTERET LAY BELOW DECKS NEAR DEATH, THE TOWN OF NEW YORK EMERGED FROM THE GLOOM. ANDROS' MEN TOOK HIM TO THE OLD FORT AND THREW HIM INTO PRISON.

THE ILLUSTRATED HISTORY OF UNION County...
by FRANK THORNE

WHEN JAMES BOLLEN AND ROBERT VANQUELLEN, CARTERET LOYALISTS, LEARNED OF THE GOVERNOR'S CAPTURE, THEY IMMEDIATELY WENT TO CARTERET'S HOME AND GATHERED HIS DOCUMENTS BEFORE ANDROS COULD SEIZE THEM.

BOLLEN AND VANQUELLEN QUICKLY LEFT TOWN AND BOOKED PASSAGE TO ENGLAND TO REPORT THE INCIDENT.

DAYS LATER A CONTINGENT OF ANDROS' TROOPS ARRIVED IN ELIZABETHTOWN AND TRIED TO ENFORCE ANDROS' RULINGS.

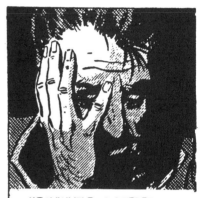

MEANWHILE, CARTERET, A SICK AND DISCOURAGED MAN, LAY IN PRISON IN OLD NEW YORK TOWN.

THE PLANTERS OF ELIZABETHTOWN WERE ENRAGED AT THIS OUTBURST OF TYRANNY BY GOVERNOR ANDROS! EVEN WITH THE INTIMIDATING PRESENCE OF THE NEW YORK TROOPS THEY SPOKE OUT AGAINST THE USURPATION AND REJECTED HIS RULE, TEARING DOWN HIS POSTED EDICTS. THEN WORD REACHED THE SETTLEMENT THAT CARTERET WAS TO BE PLACED ON TRIAL FOR OVERSTEPPING HIS BOUNDS DURING HIS RULE OF NEW JERSEY.

UNION County...

CARTERET, BEFORE A SPECIAL COURT IN NEW YORK, WAS CHARGED WITH CONTRAVENING HIS POWER AS GOVERNOR. HE WAS FOUND NOT GUILTY, BUT STRIPPED OF HIS ADMINISTRATIVE AUTHORITY.

ON HIS RELEASE, PHILIP CARTERET AND HIS YOUNG WIFE, TOOK UP RESIDENCE ONCE AGAIN IN THEIR PLANTATION MANOR. BUT HE WAS A BROKEN MAN IN DECLINING HEALTH. IN TWO SHORT YEARS HE WAS DEAD, AND ONE OF THE MOST BIZARRE CHAPTERS IN UNION COUNTY'S HISTORY HAD CONCLUDED!

SOME WEEKS AFTER THE DECISION THE SETTLERS WITNESSED GOVERNOR ANDROS ESCORT CARTERET BACK TO HIS HOME (SEE MAP 'A') IN ELIZABETHTOWN. ANDROS MADE IT A SHOW OF GRAND POMP AND CEREMONY. AS A FINAL HUMILIATION AND DEMONSTRATION OF HIS POWER, ANDROS ORDERED CARTERET SPEND SEVERAL ADDITIONAL WEEKS IN CONFINEMENT IN THE ELIZABETHTOWN JAIL!

UNION County...

by FRANK THORNE

AS THE PLANTATIONS OF UNION COUNTY GREW IN SIZE AND NUMBER MORE WORKERS HAD TO BE BROUGHT IN TO WORK THE LAND AND MAINTAIN THE LIVESTOCK.

SOME WEALTHY PLANTERS HAD AS MANY AS 20 SLAVES. MANY WERE AFRICAN AMERICAN BUT SOME WERE NATIVE AMERICANS.

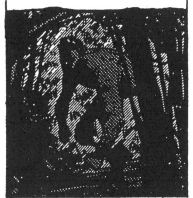

OCCASIONALLY A LABORER WOULD RUN AWAY TO FIND FREEDOM IN THE FOREST.

FEW THAT ESCAPED REMAINED FREE FOR LONG, FOR THEIR MASTERS WOULD HAVE THEM PURSUED.

SLAVES WOULD OCCASIONALLY TRY TO SELL GOODS TO SETTLERS, BUT THE SETTLERS WERE WARY, FEARING THAT THEY WERE OFFERING ITEMS STOLEN FROM THEIR MASTERS. SOME FARM WORKERS WERE FROM ENGLAND AND GERMANY, IN SERVICE UNDER CONTRACT WITH THE PLANTERS. THEY WOULD WORK FOR A PERIOD OF UP TO SEVEN YEARS IN TURN FOR PAYMENT OF THEIR PASSSAGE. SOME WERE CONVICTS DEPORTED TO THE COLONIES, OTHERS WERE FLEEING RELIGIOUS PERSECUTION.

THE ILLUSTRATED HISTORY OF UNION County...
by FRANK THORNE

Elizabethtown

THE QUAKERS ARRIVED IN ELIZABETH-TOWN IN 1685. THEY FOUND A THRIVING SETTLEMENT OF SOME 150 HOMES AND OVER 700 INHABITANTS.

THEY WERE APPALLED AT SEEING BOTH AFRICAN AMERICANS AND NATIVE AMERICANS IN SERVITUDE.

THE QUAKERS DISAPPROVED OF THE PRACTICE OF SLAVERY, AND SPOKE OUT AGAINST IT.

THE QUAKERS URGED LEGISLATION TO ABOLISH THE SHAMEFUL PRACTICE.

THAT WAS NOT TO COME IN THE LIVES OF THOSE EARLY ADVOCATES OF ABOLITION. MEANWHILE, TO THE FURTHER DISTRESS OF THE QUAKERS, SEVERAL TIMES EACH MONTH THERE WAS A *SLAVE MARKET* OPERATING AT THE ELIZABETHTOWN POINT. LONG-KEELED SAILING SHIPS WOULD BRING AFRICANS FROM ABROAD SO THAT THE PLANTERS COULD MAKE A PURCHASE. A ROBUST MALE WAS A PRIME INVESTMENT, SO EXTREME CARE WAS TAKEN IN THE SELECTION.

THE ILLUSTRATED HISTORY OF UNION County...
by FRANK HOWE

AS EARLY AS 1683 A BUSTLING PUBLIC MARKET WAS OPERATING ON WHAT IS NOW BROAD STREET IN THE AREA OF THE COUNTY COURTHOUSE. TOWNSFOLK WOULD BUY, SELL WHILE DISCUSSING THE PROBLEMS OF THE MOMENT.

BEHIND THE MEETING HOUSE WAS THE ELIZABETHTOWN GRAVEYARD.

THEY WOULD SAUNTER OVER TO THE TOWN HOUSE, WHERE NOW STANDS THE FIRST PRESBYTERIAN CHURCH.

IN TWO SHORT DECADES THE CEMETERY HAD BECOME AMPLY FULL OF GRAVESITES.

THESE RESTING SOULS HAD HELPED MAKE ELIZABETHTOWN THE MOST CULTURAL SETTLEMENT IN ALL OF NEW JERSEY. ITS FARMS WERE UNMATCHED FOR SIZE AND PRODUCTIVITY, AND THE NUMBER AND QUALITY OF ITS LIVESTOCK WAS THE ENVY OF THE EAST COAST. ONE CAN ONLY IMAGINE THEIR REACTION IF THEY WERE TO SEE ELIZABETH TODAY!

THE ILLUSTRATED HISTORY OF UNION County

by FRANK HOWE

Elizabethtown

SUNDAY MORNINGS WOULD FIND THE FAMILIES GATHERING AT THE TOWN HOUSE FOR RELIGIOUS SERVICES. SOME TREKKED CONSIDERABLE DISTANCES AND EXTREMES OF WEATHER TO WORSHIP.

IF IT WERE A WINTER'S DAY THEY WOULD COME PREPARED. MANY BROUGHT BLANKETS.

LADIES OFTEN USED FOOT STOVES AND HAND WARMERS TO FIGHT THE COLD.

OFTEN THE MINISTER'S SERMON WOULD DRONE ON FOR THREE FROSTY HOURS.

PRAYERS COULD LENGTHEN THE SERVICE TWO MORE HOURS. ADD TO THAT THE SOCIAL ACTIVITIES AND THE SABBATH PROCEEDINGS WOULD CONSUME MOST OF THE DAY. DURING THE WARM SUMMER MONTHS SOME OF THE FAITHFUL WOULD TEND TO NOD OFF. A CHURCH MEMBER WAS ASSIGNED THE TASK OF WIELDING A LONG POLE WITH A FEATHER ATTACHED TO TICKLE THE HEAVY-EYED CONGREGANT'S NOSE OR EAR AND RESTORE THE OFFENDER'S PROPER ATTENTION.

THE ILLUSTRATED HISTORY OF UNION County...
by FRANK PTAK

Elizabethtown

ON THIS BRIGHT SUMMER MORNING IN ELIZABETHTOWN A YOUNGSTER IS BEING BROUGHT TO THE HOME OF THE TOWN CONSTABLE.

A NEIGHBOR OVERHEARD THE RASCAL 'CUSSING' WHILE DOING HIS CHORES.

THE PENALTY FOR SUCH BEHAVIOR, IF THE OFFENDER IS UNDER 12, IS A FLOGGING.

FOR OLDER LAW-BREAKERS THE PUNISHMENT IS MORE EMBARRASSING.

Sweari

THIS POOR FELLOW WAS CAUGHT USING THE LORD'S NAME IN VAIN. THE INCIDENT WAS REPORTED TO THE TOWN CONSTABLE AND HE WAS APPREHENDED. THE ACCUSED WAS GIVEN THE CHOICE OF A FINE OR IMPRISONMENT IN THE STOCKS, WHICH STOOD ON WHAT IS NOW BROAD STREET NEAR THE FIRST PRESBYTERIAN CHURCH. THE BLASPHEMER WAS SHORT OF CASH SO HE CHOSE THE LATTER, AND SUFFERED FOUR HOURS OF PUBLIC HUMILIATION.

THE ILLUSTRATED HISTORY OF
UNION County...
BY FRANK HOLMES

Elizabethtown

THE ROADS THAT LED FROM THE ELIZABETHTOWN SETTLEMENT WERE HARDLY MORE THAN DIRT TRAILS. TRAVEL WAS COMMONLY SLOW, DUSTY OR MUDDY, AND FREQUENTLY TORTUOUS.

SLOW-MOVING WAGONS IN THE FOREST WERE OFTEN TARGETS FOR CRIMINALS.

IF CAUGHT, THE FELON WAS DELIVERED TO THE TOWN CONSTABLE, WHO DELIVERED A SEVERE JUDGMENT.

IF IT WAS HIS FIRST OFFENSE THE LETTER "T" WOULD BE BURNED INTO THE BACK OF HIS HAND.

IN THE CASE OF A SECOND OFFENSE HE WAS BRANDED WITH THE LETTER "B" ON HIS FOREHEAD. THE WRONGDOER NOW SPORTED A "T" FOR 'THIEF' ON HIS HAND, AND A "B" MEANING 'BURGLAR' ON HIS FOREHEAD. IT WOULD BE REMINDER ENOUGH THAT IF HE WERE TO PURSUE HIS CRIMINAL WAYS HIS THIRD OFFENSE WAS TO BE HUNG BY THE NECK UNTIL DEAD!

THE ILLUSTRATED HISTORY OF UNION County...!

by FRANK *HOWE*

Elizabethtown

THERE WERE MANY HANDSOME YOUNG MEN AND ATTRACTIVE MISSES IN OLD ELIZABETHTOWN. AND NOT A FEW OF THOSE YOUNG LADIES HAD THEIR CAPS SET TO CATCH A PROSPECTIVE SUITOR.

SUCH BRAZEN ACTIVITIES HAD NOT GONE UNNOTICED BY THE STRICT FEMALE LEGISLATORS. THEY JUDGED IT A CAPITAL OFFENSE FOR A FEMALE TO SEEK A TOWNSMAN'S ADMIRATION BY FEMININE WILES THROUGH DECEPTION AND ARTIFICIAL MEANS.

SPECIFICALLY, ANY FEMALE FOUND USING SCENTS, COSMETICS, WASHES, PAINTS, ARTIFICIAL TEETH OR BOSOMS, NON-NATURAL HAIR, OR HIGH HEEL SHOES TO BETRAY AN UNSUSPECTING MALE INTO MARRIAGE WOULD BE *PUT TO DEATH!* WITH THE GROWTH OF THE OLD TOWN CAME THE INFLUX OF MANY WEALTHY NEW YORK FAMILIES WITH HANDSOME BACHELOR SONS, OFFERING PLENTY OF OPPORTUNITY FOR AN AMOROUS YOUNG LADY TO DISPLAY HER CHARMS.

THE ILLUSTRATED HISTORY OF UNION County...

by FRANK HOWE

MANY AN ADVENTUROUS HUNTER FOLLOWED THE NARROW INDIAN TRAILS THAT WOUND THROUGH THE FIELDS AND FORESTS AROUND ELIZABETHTOWN.

OFTEN THE EXPLORER WOULD COME UPON A RIVERSIDE INDIAN VILLAGE. THE NATIVES USED THE WATERWAYS AS THEIR 'HIGHWAY.' THEY WOULD KEEP THE ENCAMPMENT FOR TEN YEARS OR SO, THEN MOVE ON TO ANOTHER SITE. THE LENNI LENAPE, WHO WERE ALSO KNOWN AS THE UNAMIS, WERE GENERALLY PEACEABLE FOLK. TO THE NORTH DWELT THE POWERFUL IROQUOIS NATION WHO TOOK ADVANTAGE OF THE LENAPE SUBMISSIVENESS BY DEMANDING TRIBUTE TO SPARE THEM FROM ATTACK.

THE ILLUSTRATED HISTORY OF UNION County...

by FRANK THORNE

BY NECESSITY THE FARMERS HAD TO BE VERSATILE. THIS JACK-OF-ALL-TRADES WAS A PROFICIENT BLACKSMITH AND WOODCARVER, AMONG MANY OTHER SKILLS.

THE TOWNSFOLK WERE A SUPERSTITIOUS LOT; ANY UNUSUAL ACTIONS WERE VIEWED WITH SUSPICION.

THE FEAR OF WITCHCRAFT PREVAILED. ANY OLD WOMAN COULD BE SUSPECT.

SOME DREADED THE "EVIL EYE" THAT WITCHES WERE KNOWN TO CAST.

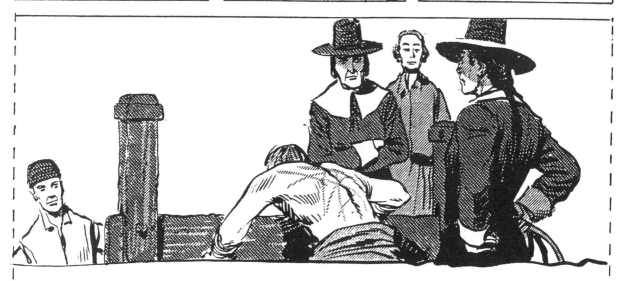

IF CONVICTED, THE PENALTY FOR PRACTICING WITCHCRAFT WAS DEATH. FORTUNATELY FOR THIS NE'ER-DO-WELL HE ONLY RECEIVED TEN "STRIPES" ON HIS BACK FOR STEALING A BOAT. IRRESPONSIBLE TALKERS, SUCH AS SLANDERERS AND COMMON SCOLDS, WERE ROUTINELY DUNKED IN A POND AS PUNISHMENT. BUT THE SENTENCE IN CASES OF COUNTERFEITING, BEARING FALSE WITNESS OR TAKING ANOTHER MAN'S WIFE WAS DEATH BY HANGING!

THE ILLUSTRATED HISTORY OF
UNION County...
by FRANK DUROSE

THERE WAS MUCH WORK TO BE DONE, SO THE TOWNSFOLK WOULD COMBINE WORK WITH PLAY. THIS FARMER IS BEING FORMALLY INVITED TO A "CORN-HUSKIN' BEE."

EVERYBODY WORKED TOGETHER AT THE "BEES." THEY WERE JOYOUS RURAL WORK PARTIES.

THERE WERE "APPLE-PICKIN' BEES," "THRASHIN' BEES," AND MANY OTHERS.

THESE LADIES ARE GOING TO A "QUILTING BEE" AT A NEIGHBOR'S FARM HOME.

QUILTING PARTIES WERE MORE COMMON IN THE LONG COLD WINTERS WHEN THERE WAS LITTLE OUTDOOR WORK. THE WINTRY MONTHS OFFERED MORE FREE TIME FOR RECREATION. WHAT BETTER FUN THAN SKATING, SLEIGH RIDING, AND SNOWBALL FIGHTS? BUT THERE WERE WARM WEATHER SPORTS TOO. THE GOOD FOLK OF ELIZABETHTOWN ENJOYED HORSE RACING, CRICKET, WRESTLING, BOXING, AND SHOOTING. MOST COLONISTS WERE EXCELLENT MARKSMEN.

THE ILLUSTRATED HISTORY OF UNION County...

by FRANK HOWE

Elizabethtown

THE *ITINERANT PEDDLER* WAS A COMMON SIGHT. HE TRAVELED FROM VILLAGE TO VILLAGE SELLING HIS WARES. HE HAD READY CUSTOMERS BECAUSE OF THE CONVENIENCE OF HIS SERVICE.

THEY CARRIED THEIR GOODS BY WAGON, CARRIAGE, HORSE OR ON FOOT.

LIKE MOST OF HIS KIND, HE WAS UNTRUSTWORTHY. HE ENTERED IF NO ONE WAS HOME AND THE DOOR WAS UNLOCKED,

ONCE INSIDE HE TOOK WHATEVER HE COULD SELL TO THE FOLK IN THE NEXT VILLAGE.

HE THEN HURRIED ON HIS WAY. THIS PRACTICE CAME TO THE ATTENTION OF THE GENERAL ASSEMBLY. THEY FRAMED A LAW THAT PEDDLERS MUST OBTAIN A WARRANT OF GOOD CHARACTER FROM THE JUSTICE OF THE PEACE. FURTHERMORE, THE PEDDLER MUST POST A BOND WITH THE COURT CLERK. AS TIME WENT ON THE ASSEMBLY LEVIED HEAVY TAXES ON THE TRAVELING MERCHANTS. EVEN SO THE TRANSIENTS BECAME A FAMILIAR SIGHT IN OLD ELIZABETHTOWN.

THE ILLUSTRATED HISTORY OF UNION County...

by FRANK THORNE

THE NEWS TRAVELED FAST WHEN IT WAS LEARNED THAT THE "MEDICINE MAN" WAS COMING TO ELIZABETHTOWN. IT WAS ANTICIPATED AS WE WOULD LOOK FORWARD TO A MOVIE.

THE LOUD BLASTS FROM A HORN BROUGHT EAGER VILLAGERS FROM MILES AROUND.

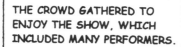

THE CROWD GATHERED TO ENJOY THE SHOW, WHICH INCLUDED MANY PERFORMERS.

MAGICIANS, PUPPETEERS, SINGERS AND ACROBATS WERE ON DISPLAY.

ALL OF THE HOOPLA AND THEATRICS SERVED THE PURPOSE OF THE SHOWMAN HIMSELF; A QUACK DOCTOR WHOSE SOLE PURPOSE WAS TO SELL TO THE UNWARY BUMPKINS VARIOUS CURE-ALL POTIONS. HE WAS INDEED THE MASTER PERFORMER. "HERE THE SECRET ELIXIR FORMULATED FROM A SECRET MIXTURE OF HERBS AND PALLIATIVES OBTAINED FROM FAR EASTERN PHARMACOPEIAS GUARANTEED TO RESTORE HEALTH AND VITALITY. YOURS FOR THE MERE COST OF THE EQUIVALENT OF A HALF BUSHEL OF TURNIPS!" AS YEARS WENT BY LAWS WERE PASSED TO CURB THE BOGUS MEDICINE SHOWS.

THE ILLUSTRATED HISTORY OF UNION County...

by FRANK HOWE

IN THE YEAR 1720 *PETER WILCOXIE* BUILT A HOME ON THE BLUFF OVER-LOOKING BLUE BROOK IN WHAT IS NOW CALLED "THE DESERTED VILLAGE" IN NEW PROVIDENCE BELOW SURPRISE LAKE.

SETTLERS WERE RAPIDLY MOVING WEST FROM ELIZABETHTOWN TOWARD THE MOUNTAINS.

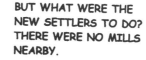

BUT WHAT WERE THE NEW SETTLERS TO DO? THERE WERE NO MILLS NEARBY.

PETER KNEW THERE WERE MILLS APLENTY NEAR ELIZABETHTOWN.

WILCOXIE, A PROGRESSIVE AND ENERGETIC MAN, STOOD AT THE RIVER'S EDGE BELOW HIS HOME AND GAZED AT A BEAVER DAM. HERE HE RESOLVED TO BUILD A MILL TO SERVE THE NEW ARRIVALS TO THE AREA. HE SET OUT THE NEXT DAY ON HORSEBACK FOR ELIZABETHTOWN TO ARRANGE FOR MACHINERY AND CONSTRUCTION MATERIALS FOR HIS MILL.

THE ILLUSTRATED HISTORY OF
UNION County...
by FRANK HOWE

AS WILCOXIE RODE EAST DOWN THE MOUNTAIN HE PASSED A GROUP OF INDIANS. THEY HAD A SIZABLE VILLAGE NEAR PETER'S HOME.

THE INDIAN TRAILS, WHICH WERE OFTEN NARROW AND INDIRECT, WOULD HAVE TO BE WIDENED TO ALLOW WAGONS TO REACH HIS MILL.

THIS MEANT SPECIAL EQUIPMENT AND EXTRA LABORERS HAD TO BE BROUGHT TO THE AREA.

IT WAS NO SMALL TASK TO GET A MILL UP AND RUNNING AND THE COST WOULD BE CONSIDERABLE.

AS PETER RODE THROUGH THE VALLEY AND UP THE WESTERN SLOPE HE APPROACHED THE BADGLEY FARM. JOHN AND PHOEBE BADGLEY HAD SETTLED IN THE MOUNTAINS AT THE SAME TIME AS PETER, SO WHEN JOHN SPOTTED PETER COMING ALONG THE TRAIL HE GREETED HIM A BROAD SMILE AND A FIRM HAND-SHAKE. AFTER THE USUAL EXCHANGE ABOUT THE WEATHER AND THE PITFALLS AND TRIUMPHS OF FRONTIER LIVING, JOHN ASKED PETER IF HE COULD SPARE A MOMENT TO SEE AN INTERESTING SIGHT.

THE ILLUSTRATED HISTORY OF UNION County...

by FRANK *(signature)*

JOHN BADGLEY LED HIS FRIEND PETER ALONG THE LOWER SLOPE TO AN *ABANDONED MINE* THAT WAS LOCATED ON HIS PROPERTY BETWEEN THE FIRST AND SECOND MOUNTAIN.

JOHN HAD LEARNED THAT MANY YEARS BEFORE THE ARRIVAL OF THE ENGLISH SETTLERS, *DUTCH PROSPECTORS* CAME TO THE WATCHUNG RANGE TO STUDY THE ROCK FORMATIONS IN HOPE OF FINDING A SOURCE OF COPPER-BEARING ORE. COPPER, THE FIRST METAL TO BE USED BY HUMANS, AND SECOND ONLY TO IRON IN ITS UTILITY THROUGH THE AGES, WAS A VALUABLE COMMODITY. THE DUTCH WERE HAPPY TO FIND IT IN THE TRAP ROCK FORMATION, SO THEY BEGAN A MINING OPERATION. CRUDE ROADS WERE CUT THROUGH THE FOREST SO OXCARTS COULD HAUL THE ORE TO BERGEN POINT. FOR A SEASON THEY TOILED, BUT AS WINTER DREW NEAR THE OPERATION WAS HALTED DUE TO INEXPERIENCED LABOR AND LACK OF FUNDS. *THE OLD COPPER MINE IS STILL IN EVIDENCE TO THIS DAY.*

THE ILLUSTRATED HISTORY OF UNION County...
by FRANK

WILCOXIE SOON HAD HIS MILL UP AND RUNNING, AND IF YOU HAD A BAG OF GRAIN TO GO THROUGH PETER'S STONES YOU ONLY NEED TOTE IT THERE BY MULE, HORSE, OR SHANK'S MARE.

IN THESE ISOLATED PARTS FLOUR AND GRIST COULDN'T BE PROPERLY MILLED BY HAND.

ONLY A MILL AND A COMPETENT MILLER COULD DO THE JOB.

YOU'D FIND HIM WAITING AT THE MILL DOOR FOR YOUR TRADE. PETER'S INVESTMENT HAD PAID OFF.

"WELL DONE," SAYS ISAAC SAYER AS HE FEELS THE TEXTURE OF HIS FLOUR. ISAAC SETTLED NEARBY AND LIKE MOST OF THE FAMILIES IN THE AREA REGULARLY BROUGHT HIS GRAIN TO THE WILCOXIE MILL. PETER RECEIVED ONE SIXTEENTH OF ALL THE GRAIN HE MILLED, AND ONE TWELFTH OF THE CORN. MUCH OF THE BUSINESS DONE IN OLD UNION COUNTY WAS THROUGH THE BARTER SYSTEM.

THE ILLUSTRATED HISTORY OF UNION County...

by FRANK THORNE

THE DOOR OF THE MEETING HOUSE SERVED THE FOLKS OF ELIZABETHTOWN MUCH LIKE THE TV NEWS WE WATCH TODAY. PUBLIC ANNOUNCEMENTS WERE POSTED AND EACH WEEK A COPY OF *THE NEW YORK GAZETTE* APPEARED.

ALL THROUGH THE WEEK THE SETTLERS WOULD STOP BY THE 'BULLETIN BOARD' TO GET THE LATEST NEWS.

THE TOWNSPEOPLE WERE PROUD THAT THE GAZETTE WAS PRINTED ON PAPER MADE IN ELIZABETHTOWN!

MANY COULDN'T READ, SO THEY WAITED UNTIL SUNDAY TO HAVE IT READ TO THEM.

THAT IS, IF THEY HADN'T HEARD THE NEWS ABOUT ALREADY THROUGH WORD OF MOUTH. NEWS TRAVELED SURPRISINGLY FAST IN COLONIAL TIMES. BUT MUCH OF THE TALK WAS IDLE GOSSIP, SO THE LITERATE RELIED ON THE GAZETTE FOR THE FACTS, AND AS WITH TODAY'S MEDIA THEY HAD TO ENDURE *COMMERCIALS!* PRINTED ADS FOR TAVERNS AND VARIOUS BUSINESSES IN OLD ELIZABETH-TOWN REGULARLY APPEARED, ALONG WITH PUBLIC NOTICES CONCERNING AUCTIONS AND DESCRIPTIONS OF RUNAWAY SLAVES. BUT THINK OF IT: *NO CARTOONS!*

THE ILLUSTRATED HISTORY OF

UNION County...

by FRANK THORNE

Elizabethtown

THE TOWN CRIER PLODS ALONG THE DUSTY LANES OF OLD ELIZABETHTOWN. AS HE CALLS THE TIME AND KEEPS A WARY EYE FOR WRONGDOERS HE HARBORS DEEP THOUGHTS OF A TERRIBLE INCIDENT.

HE MOVES THROUGH THE TOWN CENTER AND RECALLS THAT IT WAS HERE WHERE THE INSTANCE OCCURRED.

EARLIER IN THE YEAR SEVERAL AFRICAN AMERICAN SLAVES WERE BURNED AT THE STAKE. "AN ATROCITY," HE SIGHS.

"SUCH A DISGRACE TO HUMANITY," HE MUTTERS AS HE MOVES THROUGH THE GLOOMY SQUARE.

THE OCCURRENCE IN ELIZABETHTOWN WAS LINKED TO THE RUMOR THAT SOME AFRICAN AMERICANS WERE PLOTTING TO BURN DOWN NEW YORK CITY AND MURDER THE WHITE POPULATION. PANIC SPREAD THROUGH THE CITY AND MOBS OF WHITES SEIZED SEVERAL INNOCENT SLAVES AND SET THEM ABLAZE. THE MANIA COULD NOT BE CONTAINED. IT SOON SPREAD TO NEW JERSEY AND THE RESULT WAS ONE OF THE DARKEST PASSAGES IN THE HISTORY OF UNION COUNTY.

THE ILLUSTRATED HISTORY OF UNION County...
by FRANK THORNE

Elizabethtown

AFTER A MORNING OF LOG-SPLITTING THIS SETTLER WIPES HIS BROW AND GLANCES AT AN IMPORTANT PIECE OF PAPER HE KEEPS SAFELY IN HIS BREECHES.

NO, THE LOTTERY IS NOT NEW TO OUR MODERN COUNTY. IT'S AS OLD AS COLONIAL ELIZABETHTOWN!

THE MONEY RAISED WAS USED TO REPAIR AND BUILD CHURCHES AND PARSONAGES.

SO OUR SETTLER IS OFF TO SEE IF LADY LUCK WAS ON HIS SIDE.

HE HAS TO RIDE TO THE 'POINT,' FROM THERE HE'LL TAKE THE FERRY TO SHOOTER'S ISLAND LOCATED IN THE BAY SOME TEN MILES FROM ELIZABETHTOWN, WHY DOES THE POOR FELLOW HAVE TO TRAVEL SUCH A DISTANCE? WHEN THE LOTTERY WAS FIRST INTRODUCED THE ENTHUSIASM FOR IT GOT OUT OF CONTROL. THE CONCEPT BECAME SUCH A CRAZE THAT IT BEGAN TO DEMORALIZE THE CHURCH AND SOCIETY. A LAW PUT A STOP TO IT, BUT THE WILY ENTREPRENEURS WHO RAN THE LOTTERY MOVED IT OFF SHORE, OUT OF THE REACH OF THE LAW, WHERE MANY LOTTERIES THRIVED FOR YEARS TO COME.

THE ILLUSTRATED HISTORY OF
UNION County...
by FRANK "DUTRO"

THE YEAR WAS 1750, OVER TWO DECADES BEFORE HOSTILITIES BROKE OUT BETWEEN THE COLONIES AND THE BRITISH. IT WAS JUNE WHEN COLONEL WILLIAM RICKETS' SHIP LEFT NEW YORK AND SAILED OUT INTO THE BAY.

RICKETS WAS HEADING BACK TO ELIZABETHTOWN WITH FAMILY AND FRIENDS AFTER VISITING RELATIVES IN MANHATTAN. IT WAS A CLEAR DAY AND A BRISK WIND MOVED THE SHIP SWIFTLY SOUTHEAST TOWARD THE 'POINT.' RICKETS WAS UNAWARE THAT FLYING FROM THE MASTHEAD WAS A SWALLOW-TAILED PENNANT CALLED A BURGEE. AS THEY APPROACHED THE NORTH RIVER THEY ENCOUNTERED THE BRITISH WARSHIP GREYHOUND. LIEUTENANT JOHN HOWE WAS IN COMMAND OF THE GREYHOUND. HOWE SPOTTED THE FLYING PENNANT, STEPPED TO THE SWIVEL GUN AND PREPARED TO FIRE.

THE ILLUSTRATED HISTORY OF UNION County...

by FRANK THORNE

LIEUTENANT HOWE, INTIMIDATED BY THE DEFIANT DISPLAY OF THE FLYING PENNANT, PREPARED TO FIRE A WARNING SHOT OVER THE BOW OF COLONEL RICKETS' SHIP.

HE AIMED THE SWIVEL GUN AT THE PASSING VESSEL.

HE ORDERED THE GUNNER'S MATE TO LIGHT THE FUSE.

THE BALL LANDED SPLASHED INTO THE WATER A SAFE DISTANCE FROM RICKETS' SHIP.

LIEUTENANT HOWE WATCHED AS THE SCHOONER SAILED ON TOWARD ELIZABETHTOWN POINT SEEMINGLY UNAFFECTED BY THE WARNING BLAST. ENRAGED BY THIS DISOBEDIENCE HOWE SWUNG THE GUN INTO POSITION AGAIN, BUT THIS TIME HIS AIM WAS ON TARGET. HE GAVE THE GUNNER'S MATE THE ORDER TO FIRE!

THE ILLUSTRATED HISTORY OF UNION County...

THE SOUND OF THE BLAST ECHOED ALONG THE NORTH RIVER, PUTTING TO FLIGHT A FLOCK OF GULLS. THEN HOWE TOOK AIM AGAIN AND A SECOND THUNDEROUS BLAST ROCKED THE LOWER BAY.

ON BOARD RICKETS' SCHOONER THERE WAS A SIMULTANEOUS SOUND OF *CANVAS RIPPING* AND *CRACKING WOOD* AS THE SECOND BALL SMASHED THROUGH THE MAINSAIL FOLLOWED BY A *DREADFUL SCREAM* FROM THE QUARTERDECK. THE DEADLY BALL HAD STRUCK THE HEAD OF A YOUNG NURSE WHO WAS HOLDING ONE OF RICKETS' INFANT CHILDREN. *THE WOMAN WAS KILLED INSTANTLY.* THE CHILD MIRACULOUSLY ESCAPED UNHARMED. RICKETS SAILED ON TO ELIZABETHTOWN POINT. AN INVESTIGATION FOLLOWED, AND THE GUNNER'S MATE WAS HELD ON A MURDER CHARGE, FOR HE WAS THE ONE THAT LIT THE FUSE. *THIS HORRENDOUS INCIDENT WAS ONE OF THE FIRST TO KINDLE THE FLAME OF REBELLION AGAINST BRITISH DOMINATION OF THE COLONIES.*

THE ILLUSTRATED HISTORY OF UNION County...
by FRANK HOWE

Elizabethtown

A DECADE HAS PASSED SINCE THE MURDER OF THE YOUNG NURSE, WHILE THE MEMORY OF THE TRAGIC INCIDENT STILL LINGERED NEW TROUBLES AROSE.

PUBLIC GATHERINGS WERE MARKED WITH CRITICISM AGAINST BRITISH RULE.

ENGLAND'S TROUBLE WITH FRANCE PROMPTED THE BRITISH TO CALL RECRUITS FROM THE COLONIES.

Recruits wanted

WORST OF ALL, REDCOATS WERE BEING QUARTERED AT HOMES IN ELIZABETH-TOWN!

THE PUBLIC SENTIMENT AGAINST THE BILLETING OF SOLDIERS IN LOCAL DWELLINGS GREW TO THE POINT THAT THE BRITISH ORDERED BARRACKS BE BUILT IN ELIZABETHTOWN TO HOUSE THE ENGLISH MILITARY. THEY STOOD ON THE EAST SIDE OF CHERRY STREET, NORTH OF MURRAY STREET. THE BUILDING ACCOMMODATED SOME 300 TROOPS. THE REDCOATS WERE STATIONED THERE UNTIL THE FIGHTING BEGAN. THE BARRACKS HAD A DEMORALIZING EFFECT ON THE TOWNSPEOPLE, AND DID LITTLE TO SOOTHE THE RESENTMENT TOWARD THE MOTHER COUNTRY. *THE STORM CLOUDS OF WAR WERE GATHERING!*

THE ILLUSTRATED HISTORY OF
UNION County...
by FRANK SHOWE

Elizabethtown

ONE SHADOWY NIGHT IN DECEMBER A YOUNG MAN MOVES QUICKLY ALONG THE BACK TRAILS OF ELIZABETHTOWN. HE HAS TO AVOID DETECTION BY THE REDCOATS QUARTERED NEARBY.

ALL SUSPICIOUS ACTIONS WERE QUESTIONED SINCE THE COLONIES BITTERLY OPPOSED THE *STAMP ACT*.

HE MAKES HIS WAY TO A SECLUDED STOREHOUSE AT THE 'POINT,' KNOCKS, AND GIVES THE PASSWORD.

INSIDE HE IS GREETED WARMLY. IT'S A MEETING OF *THE SONS OF LIBERTY*.

THE SECRET ORGANIZATION WAS RECENTLY FORMED BY FREEDOM-LOVING COLONISTS TO LAY PLANS FOR RESISTANCE TO THE STAMP ACT. THEY WERE PATRIOTS WHO HAD FREQUENT CLANDESTINE MEETINGS TO DISCUSS HOW THEY COULD PREVENT THE KING'S STAMPS FROM BEING DISTRIBUTED IN TOWN. THE STAMPS REPRESENTED THE *FIRST TAX* IMPOSED BY BRITAIN ON THE COLONIES. THE REVENUE FROM THE STAMPS WAS USED TO HELP COVER THE COST OF MAINTAINING THE TROOPS IN THE SETTLEMENTS. *THEY WERE THE SYMBOL OF EVERYTHING THE PATRIOTS HATED ABOUT ENGLAND.*

THE ILLUSTRATED HISTORY OF UNION County...

by FRANK SHOW

THE BRITISH PARLIAMENT ORDERED THAT THE STAMPS BE PURCHASED AND PLACED ON ALL LEGAL DOCUMENTS AS WELL AS PRINTED MATERIAL SUCH AS NEWSPAPERS AND PAMPHLETS. THE PATRIOTS ARGUED THAT *THE COLONISTS HAD NO VOICE IN ELECTING MEMBERS OF THE PARLIAMENT.*

THEY OPPOSED THE ACT CALLING IT *TAXATION WITH-OUT REPRESENTATION!*

TO DISCOURAGE THE USE OF THE KING'S STAMPS THE PATRIOTS BUILT A GALLOWS ON BROAD STREET.

IT SERVED AS A CONSTANT REMINDER TO THE BRITISH SYMPATHIZERS *NOT* TO ALLOW THE STAMPS IN TOWN.

THE STAMP ACT TOOK EFFECT NOVEMBER 1ST, 1765. IT WAS REPEALED FOUR MONTHS LATER. DURING THAT TIME NOT ONE OF THE HATED STAMPS HAD APPEARED IN ELIZABETHTOWN! THE SONS OF LIBERTY HAD DONE THEIR JOB WELL! THE FOLLOWING JUNE THE MERCHANTS AND TRADERS OF THE COUNTY GATHERED AND UNANIMOUSLY RESOLVED *TO CEASE ALL TRADE WITH ENGLAND!* THE TENSION WAS GROWING; *THE OUTCOME SEEMED INEVITABLE.*

THE ILLUSTRATED HISTORY OF UNION *County*...

by FRANK THORNE

IN 1772 AN *ORPHAN LAD* OF 15 YEARS CAME TO ELIZABETHTOWN. HE HAD BEEN A HUMBLE CLERK. HIS HOME WAS ON THE ISLAND OF NEVIS IN THE WEST INDIES.

THE TEENAGER JOURNEYED BY HORSE AND CARRIAGE TO THE LIVINGSTON HOME.

THE YOUNG MAN CARRIED WITH HIM A LETTER OF INTRODUCTION.

HE WAS TO PRESENT IT TO *WILLIAM LIVINGSTON*, A PROMINENT LAWYER IN TOWN.

HE SOUGHT TO STUDY AT THE RENOWNED GRAMMAR SCHOOL AT ELIZABETHTOWN. IT WAS KNOWN AS ONE OF THE FINEST IN THE COLONIES, OFFERING A DISTINGUISHED GROUP OF COURSES AND EXCELLENT MASTERS. THE YOUNGSTER CRAVED ADVANCE AND KNOWLEDGE. THE RIG PULLED TO A STOP AT THE LIVINGSTON ESTATE ('LIBERTY HALL' STILL STANDS ON MORRIS AVENUE), AND YOUNG *ALEXANDER HAMILTON* STEPPED OUT AND VIEWED HIS NEW HOME!

THE ILLUSTRATED HISTORY OF UNION County...

by FRANK THORNE

YOUNG HAMILTON WAS IMPRESSED BY THE BEAUTY OF THE LIVINGSTON HOME AND THE WELL-KEPT GARDENS. LIBERTY HALL WAS ONE OF THE MOST BEAUTIFUL HOMES IN ELIZABETHTOWN.

THE LAD WAS GREETED BY LIVINGSTON AND HE WAS GIVEN A GRAND TOUR OF THE ESTATE.

HAMILTON THEN MET LIVINGSTON'S WIFE, MOTHER OF HIS 13 CHILDREN.

THE TEENAGER SENSED AN AIR OF GREATNESS ABOUT HIS HOST. AND JUSTLY SO.

A FEW YEARS LATER WILLIAM LIVINGSTON WAS TO BECOME THE *FIRST GOVERNOR OF NEW JERSEY!* THE NEXT AFTERNOON, AFTER A GOOD NIGHT'S SLEEP, THE LIVINGSTONS ENTERTAINED IN THE GARDEN BEHIND LIBERTY HALL. AS THE GUESTS ARRIVED YOUNG HAMILTON WAS CALLED ASIDE AND INTRODUCED TO *ELIAS BOUDINOT* AND HIS WIFE. BOUDINOT WAS AN EXCELLENT LAWYER WHO WAS TO ATTAIN FAME AS *THE PRESIDENT OF THE CONTINENTAL CONGRESS.*

THE ILLUSTRATED HISTORY OF
UNION County...

by FRANK THORNE

Elizabethtown

ALEXANDER HAMILTON WAS OFF TO SCHOOL. HE JOURNEYED ACROSS FIELDS AND COUNTRY LANES TO THE NEWLY BUILT ACADEMY NEAR THE OLD FIRST CHURCH IN ELIZABETHTOWN.

"SUCH A PICTURESQUE TOWN," OBSERVED THE LAD. "BY FAR THE CULTURAL CENTER OF THE PROVINCE."

HE REACHED THE NEWARK ROAD AND SAW DR. BARNET CHATTING WITH FRANCIS BARBER, THE NEW SCHOOLMASTER.

THEY SURELY MET AT WIDOW GRAHAM'S TAVERN. IT STOOD ON THE CORNER OF BROAD AND E. JERSEY.

BARBER HAILED THE YOUNGSTER AND THE THREE STROLLED ALONG TOGETHER. MR. BARBER, EVER IN AN EXPANSIVE MOOD, SPOKE TO HAMILTON PROUDLY ABOUT SOME OF HIS FORMER STUDENTS. HE MENTIONED *AARON BURR* WHO HAD RECENTLY ATTENDED THE SCHOOL. "BRILLIANT," BOASTED THE SCHOOL MASTER, "HE WILL SURELY MAKE HIS MARK IN THIS WORLD." THIS WAS THE VERY SAME AARON BURR WHO WOULD *MORTALLY WOUND HAMILTON* IN A DUEL IN WEEHAWKEN THREE DECADES LATER. HAMILTON DIED THE DAY FOLLOWING THE DUEL AND WAS BURIED IN THE TRINITY CHURCHYARD IN NEW YORK CITY, ENDING THE CAREER OF ONE OF THE MOST INFLUENTIAL FOUNDING FATHERS.

THE ILLUSTRATED HISTORY OF UNION County...

by FRANK THORNE

LIBERTY HALL WAS THE GATHERING PLACE FOR THE MOST INFLUENTIAL PATRIOTS. POLITICS WAS THE USUAL TOPIC OF DISCUSSION. NEWS OF *THE BOSTON TEA PARTY* HAD RECENTLY REACHED ELIZABETHTOWN.

THE BOSTON INCIDENT WAS BUT ONE OF THE MANY ITEMS TALKED ABOUT.

ELIAS BOUDINOT WAS WORRIED ABOUT THE INCREASING NUMBER OF BRITISH SYMPATHIZERS IN TOWN.

WILLIAM PEARTREE SMITH AGREED, "A DAMN LOT OF SCALAWAGS," HE INSISTED ANGRILY.

THOSE THAT WERE LOYAL TO THE CROWN WERE A MINORITY GROUP CALLED *'TORIES.'* LIKE THE SONS OF LIBERTY THEY MET IN SECRET LOCATIONS AROUND ELIZABETHTOWN. WHEN THE PATRIOTS CUT OFF ALL TRADE DEALINGS WITH THE BRITISH THE TORIES KEPT ILLICIT COMMERCE WITH THE ENGLISH ON STATEN ISLAND. THE ISLAND, ONLY A FEW HUNDRED YARDS FROM THE 'POINT,' WAS A BRITISH STRONGHOLD. "THE ISLAND PRESENTS A CONSTANT THREAT," BOUDINOT DECLARED. "WE MUST KEEP A WATCHFUL EYE ON THAT NEST OF VIPERS!"

THE ILLUSTRATED HISTORY OF
UNION County...

by FRANK TROTTA

Elizabethtown

THINGS CONTINUED TO FESTER IN THE OLD TOWN. THE NEWS WAS OMINOUS FROM THE NEW ENGLAND AREA. TENSIONS MOUNTED AS ENEMY TROOP MOVEMENTS WERE SPOTTED ON STATEN ISLAND.

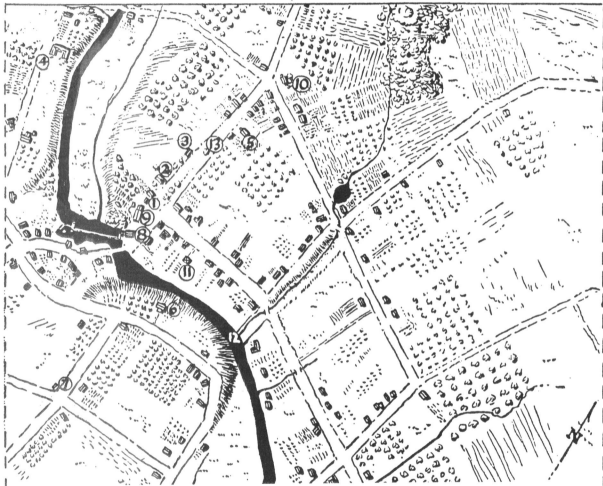

AT THE BRINK OF HOSTILITIES WE CONSIDER AN AERIAL VIEW OF ELIZABETHTOWN. FROM THIS DISTANCE IT COULD BE ANY OF THOUSANDS OF PEACEABLE COMMUNITIES IN COLONIAL AMERICA. BUT ON THOSE STREETS AND IN THOSE HOMES WERE AN ENRAGED AND DISSATISFIED PEOPLE, MOST OF WHOM CRAVED FREEDOM FROM THE DOMINATION OF THE BRITISH! (1) INDICATES THE COURT HOUSE. (2) OLD FIRST CHURCH. (3) THE ACADEMY. (4) THE ENEMY BARRACKS. (5) ST. JOHN'S CHURCH. (6) ST. JOHN'S PARSONAGE. (7) THE SCHOOLHOUSE. (8) THE MILL AT STONE BRIDGE. (9) THE RED LION INN. (10) WIDOW GRAHAM'S TAVERN. (11) THE WHITE HOUSE TAVERN. (12) THE ELIZABETH RIVER. (13) BROAD STREET.

UNION County...

by FRANK THORNE

IT WAS THE 23RD OF APRIL AT CRANE'S FERRY AT THE 'POINT' WHEN A VESSEL ARRIVED FROM NEW YORK CARRYING THE NEWS THAT *A GROUP OF PATRIOTS HAD CLASHED WITH REDCOATS AT LEXINGTON, MASSACHUSETTS.*

THERE WERE 70 MINUTE MEN AGAINST GREAT ODDS. MANY PATRIOTS WERE KILLED. *THE FIGHTING HAD BEGUN!*

THE NEWS WAS CARRIED TO EVERY VILLAGE AND FARM! *"TO ARMS!"* WAS THE CRY.

RECRUITS POURED IN FROM ALL OVER THE COUNTY TO FILL SPACES IN THE REGULAR ARMY.

WITH *THE BATTLE OF BUNKER HILL* THE COMBAT THICKENED. THE PATRIOTS OF THE COUNTY WERE GALVANIZED INTO ACTION! GENERAL WASHINGTON'S FLEDGLING ARMY NEEDED ARMS AND AMMUNITION. THE OLD WILCOXIE MILL, SECLUDED IN THE WATCHUNGS, BEGAN TO MANUFACTURE GUNPOWDER, OTHER MILLS SOON FOLLOWED SUIT. SOON ELIZABETHTOWN BEGAN SHIPPING TONS OF PRECIOUS SUPPLIES TO GENERAL WASHINGTON. *THE PATRIOTS' BLOOD WAS UP!*

UNION County

by FRANK HOWE

ON THIS *CRISP* JANUARY DAY A MESSENGER ARRIVES IN ELIZABETH-TOWN AND *GOES* DIRECTLY TO THE HEADQUARTERS OF THE FIRST JERSEY REGIMENT OF REGULARS UNDER THE COMMAND OF THE *FIERY LORD STIRLING.*

HE REPORTS TO STIRLING THAT A BRITISH TRANSPORT HAS BEEN SEEN ANCHORED OFF PERTH AMBOY.

"SHE'S LADEN WITH STORES AND SUPPLIES FOR THE RED COATS HEREABOUTS," SPOUTED THE COURIER.

WHAT A PRIZE THIS WOULD MAKE! STIRLING GATHERED 30 ARMED MEN AND THEY SET OUT FOR AMBOY.

THAT EVENING AN EXPRESS LETTER ARRIVES AT REGIMENTAL HEADQUARTERS IN ELIZABETHTOWN CARRYING DISTURBING NEWS: *A BRITISH MAN OF WAR* WITH A DETACHMENT OF MARINES AND SEAMEN HAS BEEN DISPATCHED FROM NEW YORK TO MEET THE TRANSPORT AND GUIDE IT SAFELY INTO PORT. "LORD STIRLING MUST BE WARNED," EXCLAIMED THE OFFICER IN CHARGE. "HE THINKS THE TRANSPORT IS UNPROTECTED!"

THE ILLUSTRATED HISTORY OF
UNION County..
by FRANK "HOWE"

Elizabethtown

THE REGIMENTAL COMMANDER QUICKLY DISPATCHED ONE OF HIS MEN ON THE FASTEST HORSE IN THE UNIT TO GALLOP TO AMBOY TO WARN STIRLING OF THE APPROACHING BRITISH MAN OF WAR.

VOLUNTEERS MUST BE MOBILIZED TO SAIL TO AMBOY AS REINFORCEMENTS!

THE PATRIOTS HEEDED THE CALL TO ACTION! WITH THEIR MUSKETS THEY RACED TO THE 'POINT'.

IN THE MEANTIME STIRLING ARRIVED AT AMBOY AND HAD BEGUN LOADING 100 ARMED MEN INTO THREE SHIPS.

THE CONVOY OF VOLUNTEERS SET SAIL FROM ELIZABETHTOWN POINT AND SLIPPED OFF INTO THE DARKNESS. IT MADE ITS WAY SOUTH THROUGH THE NARROW WATERS OF THE ARTHUR KILL. NO LIGHTS WERE ALLOWED ONBOARD; FOR FEAR THAT THEY WOULD BE SPOTTED BY THE BRITISH FORCES THAT OCCUPIED STATEN ISLAND. FORTUNATELY THERE WAS A GOOD BREEZE AND BY DAWN THEY SIGHTED PERTH AMBOY.

THE ILLUSTRATED HISTORY OF
UNION County...
by FRANK THORNE

Elizabethtown

THE CONVOY DOCKED AT AMBOY AND JOINED WITH STIRLING'S GROUP. STIRLING BELITTLED THE THREAT FROM THE APPROACHING BRITISH MAN OF WAR AND URGED THEY SET SAIL AND SEEK OUT THE ENGLISH TRANSPORT.

THE AMERICAN SHIPS SAILED OFF THROUGH THE ICY WATERS ON THE LOOKOUT FOR THE TRANSPORT. SOON THE CRY *"SAIL HO!"* WAS HEARD FROM THE MASTHEAD. THEY DREW NEAR, STILL WITHOUT EVIDENCE OF THE BRITISH WARSHIP. AS THE PATRIOTS BOARDED THE TRANSPORT THEY NOTED HER NAME, SHE WAS THE *BLUE MOUNTAIN VALLEY*, AND SHE SAT LOW IN THE WATER, *PROMISING A FULL CARGO OF GOODS TO AID THE REBEL MOVEMENT IN ELIZABETHTOWN!*

THE ILLUSTRATED HISTORY OF UNION County...

by FRANK THORNE

ONBOARD *THE BLUE MOUNTAIN VALLEY* THE PATRIOTS, LED BY STIRLING, CONFRONTED THE CAPTAIN WHO WAS RAILING AGAINST WHAT HE CALLED THE 'ILLEGAL ACTION.' STIRLING IGNORED HIS REMARKS AND ORDERED THAT HE BE *THROWN IN THE BRIG!*

ALL THE WHILE THEY WERE ON THE LOOKOUT FOR THE BRITISH MAN OF WAR.

BUT THERE WAS NO SIGN OF THE HEAVILY ARMED FRIGATE.

SEVERAL MILES AWAY THE WARSHIP, FAILING TO LOCATE THE TRANSPORT, SAILED BACK TO NEW YORK!

BY ORDER OF THE PATRIOTS THE SCHOONER WAS SAILED TRIUMPHANTLY UP THE SOUND BACK TO ELIZABETHTOWN POINT. SHE WAS SECURED AND HER VALUABLE CARGO OF HOGS, POTATOES, COAL, BEANS, AND SUPERB ENGLISH ALE WAS REMOVED. HER SAILS WERE REMOVED TO DISCOURAGE BRITISH RAIDING PARTIES FROM STEALING THE PRIZE AND RETURNING WITH HER TO NEW YORK.

THE ILLUSTRATED HISTORY OF UNION County by FRANK HOWE...

INDEPENDENCE!

Elizabethtown

THE DECLARATION OF INDEPENDENCE IS SIGNED IN PHILADELPHIA AND *A NATION IS BORN!* ELIZABETHTOWN WAS IN PARTICULAR DANGER BECAUSE OF THE BRITISH OCCUPATION OF NEARBY STATEN ISLAND.

WITH THE VASTLY SUPERIOR FORCES UNDER BRITISH GENERAL HOWE JUST A FURLONG AWAY, THE TOWNSMEN SET UP FORTIFICATIONS AT THE POINT. TWO CANNONS WERE SET IN PLACE AND THE MEN NERVOUSLY TOOK UP THEIR POSITIONS. SOME THOUGHT "HOW CAN OUR SHABBY FORCES DEFEAT THE GREATEST POWER ON EARTH? THE ODDS ARE A HUNDRED TO ONE!"

AT MIDNIGHT, A FEW HOURS AFTER THE DECLARATION HAD BEEN SIGNED, THE PEOPLE OF ELIZABETHTOWN WERE AWAKENED BY THE SOUND OF CANNON FIRE AT THE 'POINT.' IT WAS A DUEL BETWEEN A BRITISH SLOOP AND THE AMERICAN POSITION ON SHORE. TO THE DELIGHT OF THE GATHERING TOWNSMEN THE SLOOP WAS RIPPED TO PIECES BY THE AMERICAN SALVOS. THIS INCIDENT, OCCURRING ONLY A FEW HOURS AFTER OUR NEW NATION WAS BORN, WAS IN ALL PROBABILITY THE *FIRST MILITARY EXPLOIT OF THE UNITED STATES OF AMERICA!*

THE ILLUSTRATED HISTORY OF UNION County... by FRANK "SHOW"

Elizabethtown

SOON AFTER THE FIGHTING BEGAN WILLIAM LIVINGSTON WAS CHOSEN AS THE FIRST GOVERNOR OF NEW JERSEY. BUT TIMES WERE DARK AND THERE WERE MANY UNCERTAINTIES.

THE TORIES, WHO WERE STILL VOCAL IN THEIR OPPOSITION, CROWED ABOUT WASHINGTON'S ARMY.

"THEY ARE IN RETREAT! THEY LACK SUPPLIES AND MORALE! THE ENGLISH ARE CLOSE BEHIND!"

"SURRENDER THE TOWN TO THE BRITISH FORCE! THERE IS NO OTHER WAY!"

THAT NIGHT A MEETING OF SOME OF ELIZABETHTOWN'S MOST PROMINENT CITIZENS GATHERED IN THE HOME OF ISAAC ARNET (HIS RESIDENCE STOOD ON EAST JERSEY STREET AT THE SITE OF THE ELIZABETH CARTERET HOTEL). THE MEN WERE DEADLY SERIOUS IN THEIR DELIBERATIONS. WASHINGTON HAD SUGGESTED THEY EVACUATE THE TOWN, TAKING EVERYTHING WITH THEM THEY COULD CARRY, AND BURN THE REST. THEY MUST DECIDE EITHER TO JOIN THE ENEMY AS THE TORIES DEMAND, OR HEAD WEST TOWARD THE MOUNTAINS.

THE ILLUSTRATED HISTORY OF UNION County...

by FRANK THORNE

Elizabethtown

THE DISCUSSION CONTINUED UNTIL NEAR MIDNIGHT. "HOW CAN WE POSSIBLY WIN?" ARGUED A WEARY DEBATER. "OUR ARMY IS BEATEN AND RETREATING!"

"MUST WE LEAVE OUR HOMES TO THE MERCY OF THOSE ARROGANT TORIES?" ADDED ANOTHER CITIZEN.

"NOTHING SHORT OF THE POWER OF GOD WILL SAVE US," DECLARED A THIRD.

"I HAVE SEEN OUR ARMY. THEY ARE IN RAGS AND FIGHT WITH TOMAHAWKS AND KNIVES!"

"KNIVES AND CLUBS AGAINST MUSKETS AND CANNON. WHAT'S TO BECOME OF THEM—AND US? THE KING WILL SURELY HANG US ALL," INSISTED ANOTHER RESIDENT. "NOT SO," INTERRUPTED ANOTHER, "IF WE SURRENDER NOW THEY WILL OFFER US A FULL PARDON!" AS THEY SPOKE THEY WERE NOT AWARE THAT THEY WERE BEING OVERHEARD. A FIGURE APPEARED IN THE DOORWAY. IT WAS MRS. ARNET. HER STARE OF DISAPPROVAL SPOKE A THOUSAND WORDS OF CONDEMNATION!

THE MEN POLITELY GLANCED AT MRS. ARNET. "THIS IS NO PLACE FOR A WOMAN!" SNAPPED ONE OF THE GROUP. SHE IGNORED THE REMARK AND STEPPED INTO THE ROOM. THEN MRS. ARNET BEGAN TO SPEAK PASSIONATELY TO THE DISHEARTENED GATHERING.

THE MEN WERE SPELL-BOUND BY HER STIRRING PLEA FOR THE AMERICAN FIGHT FOR FREEDOM.

"WE WILL PREVAIL!" SHE DECLARED. THE MEN ROSE TO SALUTE HER. SHE WAS A LIGHT IN DARK TIMES.

MRS. ARNET SPOKE WITH CONVICTION OF FAITH IN GOD AND THE CAUSE THAT THE MEN WERE INSPIRED.

THE ILLUSTRATED HISTORY OF UNION County

by FRANK THORNE

Elizabethtown

THROUGHOUT THE HOSTILITIES A SURPRISING NUMBER OF BRITISH COMBATANTS WERE CAPTURED BY THE PATRIOTS. SIMILARLY, A CONSIDERABLE GROUP OF COLONIALS WERE TAKEN AS PRISONERS OF WAR.

AS THE STATE CAPITAL ELIZABETHTOWN WAS HEAVILY INVOLVED IN PRISONER EXCHANGE.

THE BRITISH WOULD BRING THEIR PRISONERS OVER TO THE 'POINT' FROM PRISONS IN STATEN ISLAND.

THEY WOULD RETURN WITH A BOATLOAD OF LIBERATED REDCOATS.

"THAT ISLAND IS A THORN IN OUR SIDE," GROWLS THIS MILITIA MAN ON WATCH AT THE 'POINT'. "THOSE BLOODY REDCOATS ARE ALL OVER THAT PLACE LIKE A SWARM OF HUNGRY JACKALS! AND YOU GOT TO WATCH 'EM, FOR NO SOONER THAN IT'S DARK OVER THEY COME ACROSS THE RIVER TO MAKE MISCHIEF. THEY'LL BE IN CAHOOTS WITH THE TORIES HERE IN TOWN; A NASTIER LOT OF SCOUNDRELS YOU'LL NOT FIND IN ALL OF THE COLONIES!"

THE ILLUSTRATED HISTORY OF
UNION County
by FRANK THORNE

Elizabethtown

AS THE NEW GOVERNOR OF A REBEL STATE, WILLIAM LIVINGSTON WAS IN CONSTANT DANGER FROM BOTH THE TORIES AND THE BRITISH FORCES IN THE AREA. IN FEBRUARY, 1779, A PLAN WAS DRAWN UP IN NEW YORK.

"WE MUST CAPTURE THIS REPROBATE THAT THE REBELS CHOOSE TO CALL THEIR GOVERNOR!"

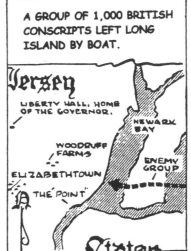

A GROUP OF 1,000 BRITISH CONSCRIPTS LEFT LONG ISLAND BY BOAT.

Jersey

LIBERTY HALL, HOME OF THE GOVERNOR.

NEWARK BAY

WOODRUFF FARMS

ENEMY GROUP

ELIZABETHTOWN

THE 'POINT'

Staten

BY 3 AM THEY PUT TO SHORE UNNOTICED AT THE MEADOWS NORTH OF THE 'POINT'.

GUIDED BY TORY TREACHERY THE GROUP MOVED INLAND. THE LEADER OF THE EXPEDITION ORDERED THAT A LOCAL BE CAPTURED SO THAT HE COULD ACCESS THE THREAT OF RESISTANCE IN THEIR ADVANCE TOWARD LIBERTY HALL. A SQUAD DRAGGED ELI HENDRICKS FROM HIS BED AND BROUGHT HIM BEFORE THEIR COMMANDING OFFICER FOR INTERROGATION. FORTUNATELY A MEMBER OF THE WOODRUFF FAMILY, WHOSE HOUSE STOOD OPPOSITE TO THE HENDRICKS' FARM, SAW THE ABDUCTION AND RACED TO TOWN TO *SPREAD THE ALARM!*

THE ILLUSTRATED HISTORY OF
UNION County...
by FRANK HOWE

Elizabethtown

WOODRUFF LOCATED GENERAL MAXWELL. "IT'S AN *INVASION!*" HE CRIED. "THERE'S GOT TO BE HUNDREDS OF THE FILTHY LOBSTER-BACKS!"

UNSURE OF THE SIZE OF THE ENEMY FORCE, MAXWELL ORDERED AN EVACUATION, AND HIS TROOPS WITHDREW.

A WISE MOVE, FOR SHORTLY ALL ROADS OUT OF TOWN WERE BLOCKED.

A SMALL DETACHMENT OF REDCOATS HEADED FOR GOVERNOR LIVINGSTON'S HOME.

THE TROOPERS APPROACHED LIBERTY HALL AND BURST THROUGH THE FRONT DOOR. THEY SEARCHED FOR THE GOVERNOR—TO NO AVAIL. LIVINGSTON WAS STAYING AT A FRIEND'S HOUSE MILES AWAY. ENRAGED, THE SOLDIERS DEMANDED THAT LIVINGSTON'S OLDEST DAUGHTER GIVE THEM HER FATHER'S PAPERS. SHE LED THEM TO HIS STUDY AND POINTED TO HIS DESK. THEY EMPTIED THE DRAWERS OF LETTERS AND DOCUMENTS AND LEFT. LATER THE BRITISH REALIZED THEY'D BEEN TRICKED. *THE MATERIAL THEY SEIZED WAS WORTHLESS!* ALL THE IMPORTANT PAPERS WERE SAFELY HIDDEN ELSEWHERE IN THE HOUSE!

THE ILLUSTRATED HISTORY OF UNION County...
by FRANK THORNE

Elizabethtown

FRUSTRATED IN THEIR ATTEMPT TO CAPTURE GOVERNOR LIVINGSTON THE REDCOAT BRIGADE CONVERGED ON ELIZABETHTOWN. THEY CAME UPON THE HOME OF PARSON CALDWELL.

THEIR TORY GUIDES ASSURED THE BRITISH COMMANDER THAT CALDWELL WAS A NOTORIOUS RABBLE-ROUSER AND A DECLARED ENEMY OF THE CROWN. THE COMMANDER ORDERED THE HOME BE TORCHED. THE EVACUEES WATCHED HELPLESSLY FROM THE EDGE OF TOWN AS THE PARSONAGE *BURNED LIKE A STACK OF STRAW.* THE INCENDIARY RAMPAGE CONTINUED AS THE BRITISH BURNED FRANCIS BARBER'S FAMOUS ACADEMY ON BROAD STREET. BY THIS TIME GENERAL MAXWELL HAD ASSESSED THE STRENGTH OF THE ENEMY FORCE AND RALLIED THE PATRIOTS TO DRIVE THE REDCOATS BACK ACROSS THE FROZEN MEADOWS TO THEIR BOATS AND OUT INTO THE FRIGID WATERS OF THE SOUND *BACK TO LONG ISLAND.*

THE ILLUSTRATED HISTORY OF
UNION *County*
by FRANK THORNE

Elizabethtown

THE MILLS OF UNION COUNTY HAD BEEN GRINDING OUT GUNPOWDER IN PREPARATION FOR AN INVASION. THE PATRIOTS WERE ONCE AND FOR ALL GOING TO DRIVE THE BRITISH FROM STATEN ISLAND!

ON JANUARY 14TH, 1780, LORD STIRLING LED 2,000 TROOPS THROUGH THREE FEET OF SNOW TO DE HART'S POINT.

THEY CROSSED THE FROZEN SOUND. AS THEY NEARED THE ISLAND IT WAS EVIDENT THAT THE BRITISH WERE HEAVILY ARMED AND WAITING.

STIRLING ORDERED A RETREAT. THE INVASION WAS A FAILURE, AND THE SEVERE COLD DISABLED MANY OF HIS TROOPS.

SHORTLY AFTER THE ABORTIVE MANEUVER A GANG OF RENEGADES FROM ELIZABETHTOWN, WITHOUT ANY MOTIVE BUT BRUTE CARNAGE AND THIEVERY, CROSSED OVER TO THE ISLAND AND LOOTED THE HOMES OF INNOCENT BRITISH CITIZENS. THE RUFFIANS SHOWED NO MERCY IN THE FORAY. *COLONEL BUSHWICK*, A TORY WHO HAD MOVED TO STATEN ISLAND, RESOLVED TO AVENGE THE ATTACKS.

THE ILLUSTRATED HISTORY OF
UNION County...
by FRANK HOWE

Elizabethtown

TEN DAYS AFTER STIRLING'S ADVANCE BUSHWICK LED A NIGHTTIME SORTIE WITH OVER 300 TORIES AND REDCOATS ACROSS THE ICE TO TREMBLY POINT, SOME 3 MILES SOUTH OF TOWN.

YOUNG *CORNELIUS HETFIELD*, AN ACTIVE TORY, LED THEM INTO ELIZABETHTOWN.

THEY MADE IT TO THE PRESBYTERIAN MEETING HOUSE WITHOUT DETECTION.

"THERE IS THE CITADEL OF THE FANATIC PARSON CALDWELL," ONE TORY TURNCOAT HISSED.

"THE SON OF A DOG PREACHES HATE! HATE OF THE CROWN AND EVERYTHING IT STANDS FOR!" ADDED ANOTHER SCOUNDREL. A THIRD ADVANCED WITH A FLAMING TORCH. "HE WANTS TO DRIVE THE LOYALISTS AND OUR ENGLISH BROTHERS INTO THE SEA!" THEN YOUNG CORNELIUS HETFIELD STEPPED FORWARD, TOOK THE TORCH AND SHOUTED "DOWN WITH THE REBEL MEETING HOUSE!"

THE ILLUSTRATED HISTORY OF
UNION County...
by FRANK THORNE

Elizabethtown

TORCH IN HAND, CORNELIUS HETFIELD APPROACHED THE FRONT DOOR. THEN THIS SON OF A RESPECTED ELIZABETHTOWN FAMILY HESITATED.

THIS WAS THE CHURCH OF HIS FOREFATHERS. HE HIMSELF HAD BEEN A MEMBER.

BUT THE BUILDING WAS BEING USED TO FAN THE FIRES OF REBELLION!

"DOWN WITH IT!" HE SCREAMED. THE TROOPERS BROKE THE DOOR DOWN.

THE FIENDISH YOUNG HETFIELD ENTERED FIRST, STILL RAGING ON HE DETAILED CALDWELL'S TRAITOROUS ACTS TOWARD THE KING. OTHERS OF BUSHWICK'S MARAUDERS FOLLOWED WITH KINDLING AND FIRE BRANDS. THE REMAINDER OF THE MOB WATCHED UNEASILY AS STREAKS OF LIGHT BEGAN TO FLICKER ON THE WINDOW PANES. THEN THE ARSONISTS FLED THE BURNING BUILDING. SOON THE HEAVENS WERE AGLOW. BUSHWICK ORDERED THE COURTHOUSE BE SET ABLAZE, THEN HE, WITH HIS BAND OF HOOLIGANS, RETREATED TO STATEN ISLAND.

THE ILLUSTRATED HISTORY OF UNION County...

by FRANK HOWE

THE NEXT MORNING PARSON CALDWELL STOOD LOOKING AT THE CHARRED REMAINS. *FIRST HIS HOME WAS BURNED, NOW HIS CHURCH.*

UNDETERRED, HE RESOLVED TO BE EVEN MORE INVOLVED WITH THE REBEL CAUSE. *BUT WHERE WOULD HE PREACH?*

THE ELDER HETFIELD JOINED HIM AT THE RUIN. THEY GREETED EACH OTHER WARMLY.

HATFIELD SENIOR WAS A RESPECTED PATRIOT, QUITE THE OPPOSITE OF HIS SON.

THE ELDER HETFIELD OFFERED AN APOLOGY. CALDWELL UNDERSTOOD HIS AGONIZING OVER HIS SON'S DESPICABLE ACTIONS. HETFIELD OFFERED THE USE OF HIS SIZEABLE STOREHOUSE FOR RELIGIOUS SERVICES. BY THE FOLLOWING SUNDAY MEMBERS OF THE CONGREGATION HAD CONSTRUCTED PEWS AND A PULPIT. HETFIELD ARRIVED AT THE CHURCH WITH SEVERAL BODYGUARDS, FOR HE WAS A MAN OF WEALTH AND AT RISK OF BEING SEIZED BY LAWLESS BANDS AND HELD FOR RANSOM. *THESE WERE DANGEROUS TIMES IN OLD ELIZABETHTOWN.* THE PARISHIONERS WELCOMED HETFIELD WITH APPLAUSE.

THE ILLUSTRATED HISTORY OF UNION County...

by FRANK HOWE rsey

Elizabethtown

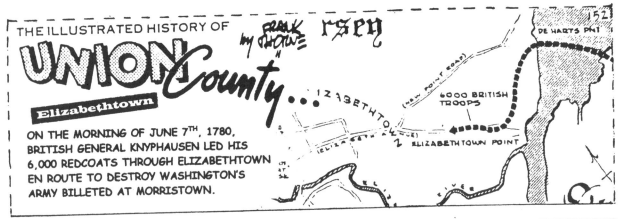

DE HARTS PNT

(NEW POINT ROAD)

6000 BRITISH TROOPS

ELIZABETHTOWN

ELIZABETHTOWN POINT

ELIZ RIVER

ON THE MORNING OF JUNE 7TH, 1780, BRITISH GENERAL KNYPHAUSEN LED HIS 6,000 REDCOATS THROUGH ELIZABETHTOWN EN ROUTE TO DESTROY WASHINGTON'S ARMY BILLETED AT MORRISTOWN.

WHAT A SPECTACLE! THE BRITISH SOLDIERS WERE STUNNING IN THEIR SCARLET UNIFORMS. A BRIGHT MORNING SUN GLINTED OFF THEIR GOLD BUTTONS AND RAZOR-SHARP BAYONETS AS THEY MARCHED IN PERFECT RANK AND STEP PAST THE CONSTRUCTION SITE OF THE NEW PRESBYTERIAN CHURCH ON BROAD STREET.

BUT THE ENEMY DID NOT PASS THROUGH THE COUNTRYSIDE UNOPPOSED. FARMERS AND TOWNSPEOPLE RALLIED ALONG THE ROUTE TO HARASS THE ADVANCING COLUMN FROM BEHIND STONE FENCES AND TREES. SOME TOOK POTSHOTS WITH THEIR 'BROWN BESS' RIFLES WHILE OTHERS THREW STONES. THE BRITISH RETURNED FIRE WITH THEIR DISMALLY INACCURATE 14 POUND MUSKETS. THE PATRIOTS WOULD MELT AWAY INTO THE UNDERBRUSH AFTER EACH ATTACK. THE REDCOATS RESOLUTELY MARCHED ON.

THE ILLUSTRATED HISTORY OF UNION County...

by FRANK THORNE

Elizabethtown

AT THE FIRST SIGHT OF THE REDCOAT COLUMN A COURIER WAS SENT FROM ELIZABETHTOWN TO CONNECTICUT FARMS TO WARN THE MILITIA OF THE APPROACHING ENEMY FORCE.

TRADITION SAYS THE LANE HE SPED ALONG WAS NAMED FOR THE EVENT: *GALLOPING HILL ROAD!*

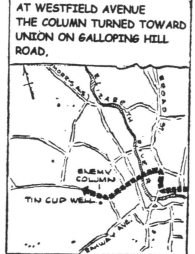

AT WESTFIELD AVENUE THE COLUMN TURNED TOWARD UNION ON GALLOPING HILL ROAD.

AS THE REDCOATS MARCHED BY, A POOR HALF-WITTED BOY WATCHED FROM A FIELD NEXT TO *TIN CUP WELL.*

A THIRSTY BRITISH SOLDIER APPROACHED AND TAUNTED THE LAD, INSISTING HE JOIN THE ROYAL TROOPERS AS A WATER BOY. THE YOUNGSTER LITTLE UNDERSTOOD, BUT THE REDCOAT PRESSED ON AND AS SEVERAL OTHER SOLDIERS JEERED, *HE TRIUMPHANTLY BAYONETED THE BOY ON THE SPOT!* THEY LEFT HIM TO BLEED TO DEATH. THE MURDEROUS ACT COULD BE SAID TO HAVE BROUGHT ILL-LUCK ON THE INVADERS, FOR THE COMBINED MILITIA TURNED THE BRITISH BACK AT UNION.

THE ILLUSTRATED HISTORY OF

UNION County...

by FRANK THORNE

IN THE BLINDING FURY OF AN ELECTRIC STORM GENERAL KNYPHAUSEN'S COLUMN RETREATED TOWARD DE HART'S POINT. THEY PASSED LIBERTY HALL. FROM INSIDE MRS. LIVINGSTON AND HER DAUGHTERS OBSERVED AN EERIE LIGHT IN THE SKY.

IT WAS THE VILLAGE OF UNION BURNING! THE GOVERNOR WAS AWAY AT MORRISTOWN.

THERE WAS A KNOCK ON THE DOOR. SEVERAL BRITISH OFFICERS REQUESTED THAT THEY STAY THE NIGHT.

OUT OF FEAR FOR HER AND HER CHILDREN'S SAFETY MRS. LIVINGSTON AGREED.

SURPRISINGLY THE LIVINGSTONS FOUND THE OFFICERS TO BE QUITE POLITE AND COURTEOUS. THEN, ABOUT MIDNIGHT, THE OFFICERS WERE CALLED AWAY TO ADDRESS UNREST AND DRUNKENNESS IN THE REDCOAT ENCAMPMENT NEARBY. LATER THE LIVINGSTONS SAW A ROWDY GROUP OF INTOXICATED SOLDIERS COME STAGGERING TOWARD LIBERTY HALL. THEY APPROACHED THE HOUSE AND WITH HORRID OATHS *BURST OPEN THE FRONT DOOR!*

THE ILLUSTRATED HISTORY OF
UNION County...
by FRANK THORNE

THE DRUNKEN BRITISH SOLDIERS STAGGERED INTO LIBERTY HALL. MRS LIVINGSTON AND HER CHILDREN WERE BARRICADED IN THE MASTER BEDROOM ON THE SECOND FLOOR. THE HOOLIGANS SOON FOUND THEIR HIDING PLACE.

THE INTRUDERS, SOT WITH STRONG DRINK, POUNDED ON THE BEDROOM DOOR DEMANDING THEY BE ADMITTED. THE MEN PERSISTED, STRIKING THE DOOR WITH THEIR FISTS. JUST AS IT WAS ABOUT TO BURST OPEN *KITTY LIVINGSTON*, THE ELDEST DAUGHTER, STEPPED FORWARD AND RESOLUTELY OPENED IT. ONE OF THE TIPSY TRESPASSERS SEIZED HER BY THE ARM. WITH QUICKNESS OF THOUGHT, SHE GRASPED HIS COAT COLLAR. AT THAT INSTANT A FLASH OF LIGHTNING ETCHED KITTY'S WHITE ROBE AND EQUALLY ASHEN FACE. THE WRETCH FELL BACK. *"GOOD GOD! IT'S MRS. CALDWELL WHOM WE KILLED THIS VERY DAY IN THE PARSONAGE AT CONNECTICUT FARMS!"* HE CRIED. THEN THE REDCOATS SHAMBLED BACK DOWN THE STAIRS AND FLED INTO THE NIGHT.

THE ILLUSTRATED HISTORY OF
UNION County...

by FRANK DICIVE

Elizabethtown

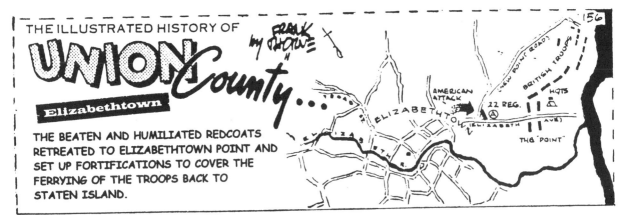

THE BEATEN AND HUMILIATED REDCOATS RETREATED TO ELIZABETHTOWN POINT AND SET UP FORTIFICATIONS TO COVER THE FERRYING OF THE TROOPS BACK TO STATEN ISLAND.

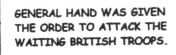

GENERAL HAND WAS GIVEN THE ORDER TO ATTACK THE WAITING BRITISH TROOPS.

THE NEXT MORNING AMERICAN SCOUTS FOUND THAT ALL BUT 500 HAD MADE THE PASSAGE.

THEY GROUPED AT TOWN CENTER AND SWEPT DOWN TOWARD THE ENEMY.

HAND'S MILITIA CAME UPON THE 22ND REGIMENT OF REGULARS AT THE CROSSROADS (UNION SQUARE 'A' ON MAP). THEY WERE MET BY FIRE FROM TWO CANNONS AS WELL AS A FIERCE HAIL OF MUSKETRY. THE AMERICANS TOOK RAPID COVER IN THE WOODS. FORTUNATELY THE AIM OF THE BRITISH WAS TOO HIGH AND THE BALLS WENT HARMLESSLY OVER THEIR HEADS. THE MILITIA THEN RETIRED TO THEIR POSITIONS AT TOWN CENTER WITHOUT THE LOSS OF A SINGLE MAN.

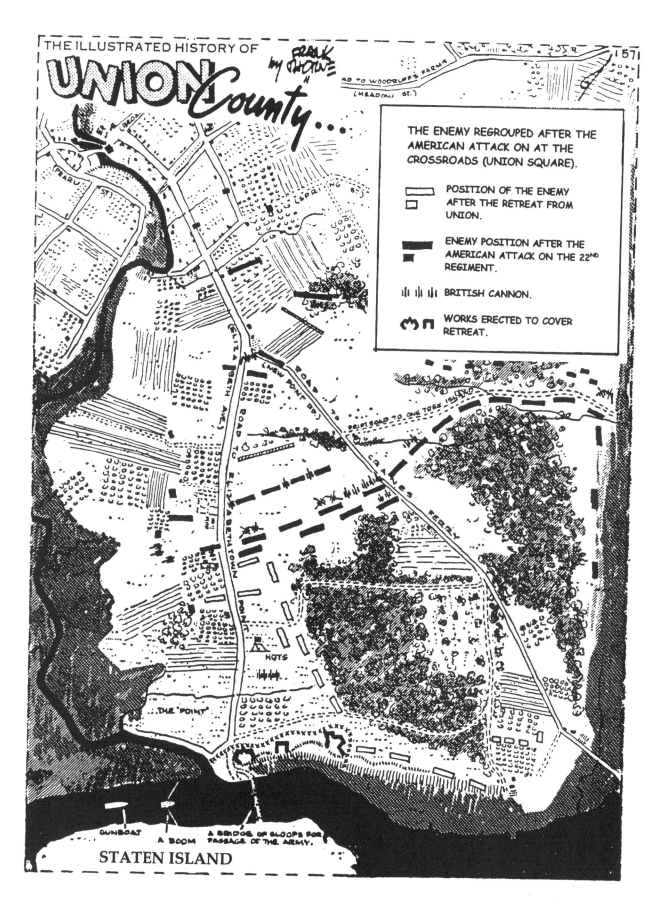

THE ILLUSTRATED HISTORY OF UNION County

by FRANK THORNE

AS THE END OF OUR TRIP BACK IN TIME DRAWS NEAR WE RETURN TO THE MOMENTOUS *BATTLE OF SPRINGFIELD* AND PRESENT THE LEGEND OF *THE UNKNOWN SOLDIER OF SPRINGFIELD.*

HE WAS A FARM BOY WITH HOPES OF JOINING THE CONTINENTAL ARMY.

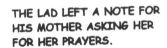

THE LAD LEFT A NOTE FOR HIS MOTHER ASKING HER FOR HER PRAYERS.

HE TREKKED LONG MILES THAT NIGHT OVER THE HILLS FROM SOMERSET.

THE YOUNGSTER WAS CERTAIN HE COULD DRUM AS WELL AS ANY IN THE MILITARY, FOR HIS MOTHER HAD GIVEN HIM A FINE DRUM FOR CHRISTMAS AND HE HAD PRACTICED DILIGENTLY. HE WAS A GOOD AND LOYAL SON WHO EAGERLY DID HIS CHORES WITHOUT COMPLAINT. BUT HE DREAMED OF MARCHING WITH THE CONTINENTALS. HE SAW HIMSELF IN LOCKSTEP WITH HIS SECTION BEATING MARTIAL TATTOOS TO STIR THE SOLDIERS TO BATTLE AGAINST THE ENEMIES OF FREEDOM!

THE ILLUSTRATED HISTORY OF UNION County...

by FRANK HOWE

THE YOUNG PATRIOT KNEW THAT GENERAL WASHINGTON AND HIS FORCES WERE SOMEWHERE IN THE HILLS ABOVE SPRINGFIELD WAITING FOR YET ANOTHER ATTACK BY THE REDCOATS FROM THEIR STRONGHOLD ON STATEN ISLAND.

HE'D FIND THE GREAT GENERAL AND BEG FOR A CHANCE TO BE A PART OF HIS DRUM CORPS.

SURELY HE'D AGREE! AND PERHAPS THE BOY COULD FIGHT AS WELL, FOR HE WAS A FINE MARKSMAN.

THEN HE HEARD THE NEARBY SOUND OF A SIGNAL GUN. HE HURRIED IN THAT DIRECTION.

AS HE SHAMBLED UP A RISE HE FELL IN BEHIND A GROUP OF MINUTEMEN WHO WERE BRISKLY WALKING ALONG A MOUNTAIN TRAIL, HEADING, HE WAS CERTAIN, FOR WASHINGTON'S ENCAMPMENT IN THE WATCHUNGS. HIS DREAM WAS COMING TRUE!

THE ILLUSTRATED HISTORY OF
UNION County
by FRANK HOLM

HIS GROUP CAME UPON A WIDE DIRT ROAD AS A TROOP OF CAVALRY THUNDERED BY HEADING TOWARD SPRINGFIELD TO TURN BACK THE ADVANCING BRITISH ARMY.

"IT'S 'LIGHT HORSE HARRY' AND HIS DRAGOONS!" SHOUTED ONE OF THE MEN.

THE BOY HAD HEARD MANY HEROIC ACCOUNTS OF MAJOR LEE AND HIS MOUNTED CAVALRY.

"THERE!" SHOUTED ONE OF THE MEN, "SPRINGFIELD LIES AHEAD!"

FROM THE SLOPE OF THE MOUNTAIN THE LAD COULD SEE THE WHITE SPIRE OF THE CHURCH. HE AND HIS FAMILY HAD WORSHIPPED THERE SEVERAL TIMES. HE KNEW THE VILLAGE WELL. OMINOUS SWIRLS OF SMOKE SPIRALED UPWARD FROM THE FIELDS SURROUNDING THE SETTLEMENT. HIS GROUP MADE IT TO THE OUTSKIRTS OF SPRINGFIELD AND JOINED WITH THE TOWN MILITIA THAT WERE POSITIONING FOR THE FIGHT.

THE ILLUSTRATED HISTORY OF
UNION County
by FRANK THORNE

IT ALL HAPPENED SO SUDDENLY! HE WAS ACTUALLY MARCHING AND BEATING HIS DRUM LIKE A VETERAN. THE FARM BOY FROM THE BLUE HILLS WAS LIVING HIS DREAM!

"THAT'S THE WAY, BOY! YOU'RE PUTTIN' GINGER IN-TO IT!" URGED A SOLDIER AT HIS SIDE.

"WHOSE COMMAND ARE WE UNDER?" THE LAD ASKED. "GENERAL GREEN, SON." REPLIED THE SOLDIER.

"HE'S SENDING US AHEAD TO MAN THE GUN AT THE BRIDGE OVER THE RIVER AT SPRINGFIELD."

"COLONEL ANGEL'S RHODE ISLANDERS ARE GUARDING IT NOW," CONTINUED THE SOLDIER. "COLONEL SHREVE WILL BE SUPPORTIN' US. HE'S AT THE BRIDGE TO THE REAR. WE'LL BE HAVIN' IT HOT AND HEAVY WHERE WE'RE GOIN'. AIN'T YOU A TAD SCARED, SON?" "NOT A BIT", REPLIED THE DRUMMER BOY. THEN HIS IMAGINATION GOT THE BEST OF HIM. "I WAS TO MIDDLEBROOK UNDER GENERAL KNOX OUT PLUCKEMIN WAY." THE OLD SOLDIER LOOKED AT HIM SKEPTICALLY. "BULLY, M' BOY!"

THE ILLUSTRATED HISTORY OF UNION County
by FRANK THORNE

"WE'LL TOMCAT THEM LOBSTER-BACKS, JUST YOU WAIT AND SEE!" BOASTED THE OLD SOLDIER. "GENERAL GREEN IS THE BEST STRAT-EE-GIST WE GOT."

"MAJOR LEE'S IN THE BATTLE TOO," ADDED THE BOY. "AND 'SCOTCH WILLIE,'" SAID THE SOLDIER. "GENERAL MAXWELL TO YOU, SON!"

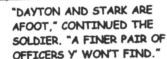

"DAYTON AND STARK ARE AFOOT," CONTINUED THE SOLDIER. "A FINER PAIR OF OFFICERS Y' WON'T FIND."

"BUT NONE OF 'EM CAN TAN THE BARK OF GENERAL GEORGE WASHINGTON!" CONCLUDED THE SOLDIER.

THE COLUMN CAME TO A HALT AT A HIGH EMBANKMENT. THE OLD SOLDIER AND THE BOY PARTED COMPANY AS EACH HAD TO SCRAMBLE UP THE SLOPE AND REPOSITION. THE YOUNGSTER WAS SPRY AND QUICK OF EYE. HE MOVED LIKE THE INDIANS HE SO MUCH ADMIRED. HE SHAMBLED DOWN THE RISE AND SAW THE BRIDGE LOOMING AHEAD THROUGH THE GATHERING SMOKE.

THE ILLUSTRATED HISTORY OF UNION County...

by FRANK THORNE

THE FARM BOY FROM THE BLUE HILLS WATCHED AS THE LOCAL MILITIA BEGAN DISMANTLING THE BRIDGE IN HOPES OF SLOWING THE ADVANCE OF THE REDCOATS,

IT WAS THE JOB OF THE TROOPS UNDER GENERAL GREEN TO GUARD THE CROSSING.

A CANNON HAD BEEN PUT IN PLACE NEARBY. SUDDENLY THE FIRING BEGAN!

A LINE OF BRITISH DRAGOONS SURGED FORWARD AS THE CANNON BOOMED.

THE MOUNTED REDCOATS THREATENED TO BREAK THROUGH THE AMERICAN DEFENSES AND ALLOW THE ENEMY COLUMN TO PASS AND PRESS ON TO DESTROY WASHINGTON'S ARMY IN THE MOUNTAINS TO THE WEST. NOW THE FIGHTING WAS EVERYWHERE; IN THE FIELDS AND ORCHARDS. MUSKETS BLAZED FROM EVERY QUARTER, BLINDING SMOKE TORE AT THE BOY'S EYES AS SHELLS BURST IN THE TREES AND ON THE ROOFS OF THE BUILDINGS NEARBY.

THE ILLUSTRATED HISTORY OF UNION County
by FRANK THORNE

CLUTCHING HIS DRUM, THE FARM BOY WATCHED IN SAFETY FROM BEHIND A LARGE BOULDER. TO HIS RIGHT THE CANNON WAS DELIVERING SALVO AFTER SALVO WITH DEADLY ACCURACY.

THE LAD SAW HIS FRIEND MANNING THE CANNON. THEN THE OLD SOLDIER GASPED AND FELL BACK.

ANOTHER TROOPER TOOK HIS PLACE. THERE WERE A SCANT 200 MEN AT THAT POSITION.

THE REDCOATS PRESSED THE ATTACK AS THE PATRIOTS CALLED FOR MORE WADDING FOR THEIR MUSKETS!

ABOVE THE NOISE OF BATTLE THE YOUNGSTER HEARD THE SOUNDS OF HOOF BEATS. HE COULDN'T BELIEVE HIS EYES. HE INSTANTLY RECOGNIZED PARSON CALDWELL. CALDWELL WAS CARRYING STACKS OF HYMNALS AND URGING THE MUSKETEERS TO USE THE PAGES AS WADDING FOR THEIR RIFLES! BACK AND FORTH THE BATTLE RAGED AS THE CANNON ROARED IN DEFIANCE. WITH WAVE AFTER WAVE OF ENEMY SOLDIERS THRUSTING FORWARD *THE BOY HEARD THE ORDER TO CHARGE!*

"COME ON! DO AND DIE FOR YOUR COUNTRY!" CAME THE CALL FROM THE STEAMING BLOOD-SOAKED BATTLEFIELD. THE FARM BOY STOOD AND BEGAN TO BEAT HIS DRUM FURIOUSLY.

IN MINUTES HE WAS IN THE MIDST OF THE DESPERATE ADVANCE.

THE TROOPER IN FRONT OF THE BOY FELL DEAD. THE LAD THREW HIS DRUM ASIDE.

HE GRABBED THE LIFELESS SOLDIER'S MUSKET AND PRESSED ON.

SUDDENLY A REDCOAT LOOMED BEFORE HIM IN THE ACRID SMOLDER OF BATTLE. THE ENEMY TROOPER WAS BARELY OUT OF HIS TEENS! THE TWO YOUNGSTERS FACED EACH OTHER FOR WHAT SEEMED AN ETERNITY. THEN THE MOUNTAIN BOY LUNGED AT THE YOUNG BRITISH CONSCRIPT WITH HIS BAYONET AT THE READY. THE TERRIFIED YOUNG ENGLISHMAN APPEARED HELPLESS TO REACT!

THE ILLUSTRATED HISTORY OF UNION County...

by FRANK THORNE

THE BLUE HILLS MOUNTAIN BOY RAN THE YOUNG REDCOAT THROUGH WITH HIS BAYONET. THE YOUNG ENEMY SOLDIER CRUMPLED BEFORE HIM AND FELL DEAD. TEARS OF TRIUMPH WELLED IN THE FARM BOY'S EYES.

THEN, SEEMINGLY ALONE, HE CHARGED ON, THE STINK OF DEATH CLUNG TO HIS NOSTRILS.

THE BOY GLANCED BACK AT THE KILLING FIELDS, BUT BEFORE HIM THE REDCOATS WERE RETREATING!

THEN THERE WAS A WHIZZING SOUND AND THE YOUNG PATRIOT WAS SLAMMED FORWARD.

AT DAYBREAK THE FOLLOWING DAY, AFTER THE TOTAL RETREAT OF THE BRITISH FORCES, THE SORRY BUSINESS OF GATHERING THE DEAD BEGAN. TWO STOIC MEMBERS OF THE TRIAGE TEAM CAME UPON THE LIFELESS BODY OF THE FARMER'S SON. "JUST A KID," REMARKED ONE OF THE MEN AS THEY ROLLED THE BODY. "DOESN'T LOOK FAMILIAR, THERE'S NO TELLIN' WHO HE WAS, BUT AT LEAST THERE'S NO FIGHTIN' WHERE HE'S GONE." HIS PARTNER HELD BACK A SOB. "WE'LL BURY HIM IN THIS GULLY ALONGSIDE THE TREE WHERE HE FELL. MAYBE SOMEONE WILL WANT TO GIVE HIM A DECENT BURIAL SOMEDAY. THERE'S NO TIME FOR IT NOW."

THE ILLUSTRATED HISTORY OF
UNION County
by FRANK THORNE

IN 1783 THE GUNS FELL SILENT AS THE PEACE ACCORD WAS SIGNED. THE WAR FOR INDEPENDENCE WAS OVER. *ENGLAND HAD SENT 60,000 SOLDIERS ACROSS THE OCEAN TO FIGHT IN AN ALIEN ENVIRONMENT AGAINST A DETERMINED POPULACE THAT CRAVED FREEDOM.*

THE JOLLY ROGER FLYING FROM THE TOPMASTS OF SHIPS ALONG THE NEW JERSEY SHORE? WELL, MAYBE THE PIRATES WHO STALKED THE UNWARY MERCHANTMEN DIDN'T ACTUALLY FLY THE SKULL AND CROSSBONES, BUT THEY WERE PIRATES NONE THE LESS. THEIR STRONGHOLDS WERE THE MANY COVES AND INLETS IN BARNEGAT BAY AND RIVERS FROM LOWER NEW YORK BAY SOUTH TO CAPE MAY POINT. IT IS CERTAIN THAT PIRATE TREASURE STILL LAYS HIDDEN IN NEW JERSEY'S SANDY SOIL. SO, THE NEXT TIME YOU STROLL THE SHORES OF THE MULLICA OR THE NAVESINK YOU MAY BE WALKING OVER BURIED *GOLD DOUBLOONS* AND *PIECES OF EIGHT!*

THE ILLUSTRATED HISTORY OF UNION County

by FRANK THORNE

THROUGH THE YEARS ELIZABETHTOWN WAS SHORTENED TO ELIZABETH, BUT HISTORY WAS STILL BEING MADE IN OUR COUNTY SEAT. IN 1819 THE BOILERS FOR THE *SAVANNAH*, THE FIRST OCEANIC STEAM BOAT, WERE MADE IN ELIZABETH.

WINFIELD SCOTT, HERO OF TWO WARS AND COMMANDER OF THE UNITED STATES ARMY, MOVED TO ELIZABETH IN THE EARLY 1800's.

BUT ALL WERE HEROES THAT FOUGHT IN THE MANY WARS THAT FOLLOWED THE WAR FOR INDEPENDENCE!

IN 1882 *ADMIRAL 'BULL' HALSEY* WAS BORN IN ELIZABETH WHERE HE SPENT MUCH OF HIS YOUTH.

THE YEAR 1898 FOCUSED THE EYES OF THE WORLD ON ELIZABETH ONCE AGAIN. *THE FIRST SUCCESSFUL SUBMARINE* WAS BUILT AT THE CRESCENT SHIPYARDS. THE *HOLLAND*, NAMED FOR NEWARK RESIDENT JOHN P. HOLLAND, THE DESIGNER AND BUILDER FAMOUS FOR DEVELOPING UNDERSEA CRAFT. HOLLAND HAD MADE TWO PREVIOUS ATTEMPTS TO CONSTRUCT A SUBMARINE, BUT THE *HOLLAND* WAS THE FIRST PRACTICAL SUBMERSIBLE. THE SUB WAS APPROVED BY THE NAVAL DEPARTMENT AND A QUANTITY WAS ORDERED TO BE PUT INTO IMMEDIATE SERVICE.

THE ILLUSTRATED HISTORY OF UNION County...

by FRANK THORNE

THIS IS THE FIRST SECTION OF
A THREE-PART MAP OF OUR COUNTY.
SHOWN IN BLACK CIRCLES ARE
HISTORIC SITES THAT STILL EXIST.
THE SMALLER LINE DRAWINGS
INDICATE LANDMARKS NO LONGER
IN EVIDENCE.

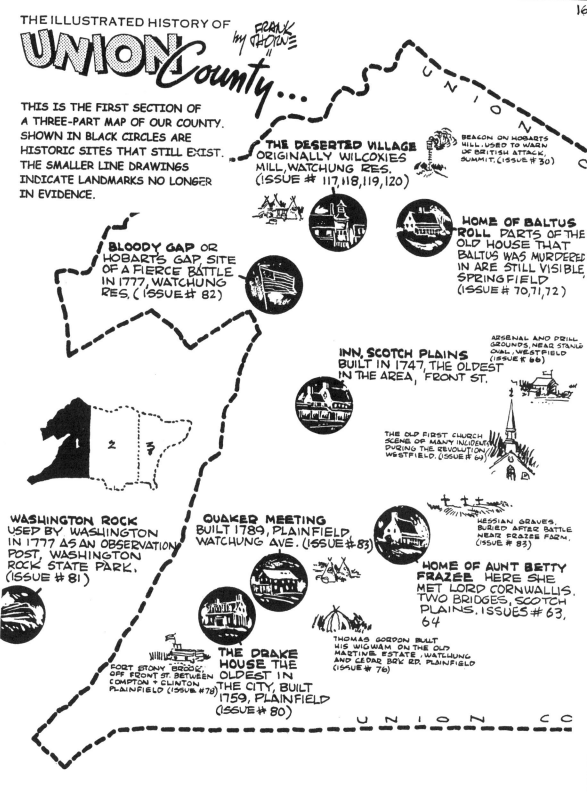

THE DESERTED VILLAGE ORIGINALLY WILCOXIES MILL, WATCHUNG RES. (ISSUE # 117, 118, 119, 120)

BEACON ON HOBARTS HILL, USED TO WARN OF BRITISH ATTACK, SUMMIT. (ISSUE # 30)

HOME OF BALTUS ROLL PARTS OF THE OLD HOUSE THAT BALTUS WAS MURDERED IN ARE STILL VISIBLE, SPRINGFIELD (ISSUE # 70, 71, 72)

BLOODY GAP OR HOBARTS GAP, SITE OF A FIERCE BATTLE IN 1777, WATCHUNG RES. (ISSUE # 82)

INN, SCOTCH PLAINS BUILT IN 1747, THE OLDEST IN THE AREA, FRONT ST.

ARSENAL AND DRILL GROUNDS, NEAR STANLEY OVAL, WESTFIELD (ISSUE # 66)

THE OLD FIRST CHURCH SCENE OF MANY INCIDENTS DURING THE REVOLUTION, WESTFIELD. (ISSUE # 64)

WASHINGTON ROCK USED BY WASHINGTON IN 1777 AS AN OBSERVATION POST, WASHINGTON ROCK STATE PARK. (ISSUE # 81)

QUAKER MEETING BUILT 1789, PLAINFIELD, WATCHUNG AVE. (ISSUE # 83)

HESSIAN GRAVES, BURIED AFTER BATTLE NEAR FRAZEE FARM, (ISSUE # 83)

HOME OF AUNT BETTY FRAZEE HERE SHE MET LORD CORNWALLIS. TWO BRIDGES, SCOTCH PLAINS. ISSUES # 63, 64

THOMAS GORDON BUILT HIS WIGWAM ON THE OLD MARTINE ESTATE, WATCHUNG AND CEDAR BRK RD. PLAINFIELD (ISSUE # 76)

FORT STONY BROOK, OFF FRONT ST. BETWEEN COMPTON + CLINTON PLAINFIELD (ISSUE #78)

THE DRAKE HOUSE THE OLDEST IN THE CITY, BUILT 1759, PLAINFIELD (ISSUE # 80)

U N I O N   C C

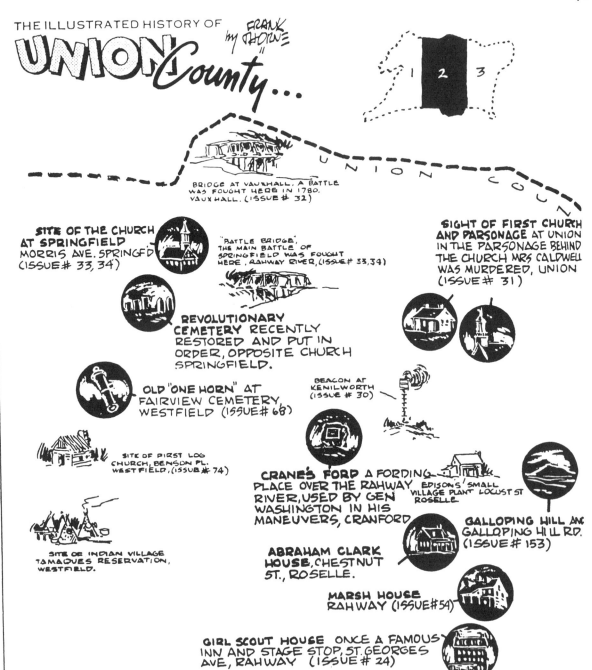

THE ILLUSTRATED HISTORY OF UNION County... by FRANK THORNE

BRIDGE AT VAUXHALL, A BATTLE WAS FOUGHT HERE IN 1780. VAUXHALL. (ISSUE # 32)

SITE OF THE CHURCH AT SPRINGFIELD MORRIS AVE. SPRINGFD (ISSUE # 33, 34)

"BATTLE BRIDGE", THE MAIN BATTLE OF SPRINGFIELD WAS FOUGHT HERE, RAHWAY RIVER, (ISSUE # 33,34)

SIGHT OF FIRST CHURCH AND PARSONAGE AT UNION IN THE PARSONAGE BEHIND THE CHURCH MRS CALDWELL WAS MURDERED, UNION (ISSUE # 31)

REVOLUTIONARY CEMETERY RECENTLY RESTORED AND PUT IN ORDER, OPPOSITE CHURCH SPRINGFIELD.

OLD "ONE HORN" AT FAIRVIEW CEMETERY WESTFIELD (ISSUE# 68)

BEACON AT KENILWORTH (ISSUE # 30)

SITE OF FIRST LOG CHURCH, BENSON PL. WESTFIELD, (ISSUE # 74)

CRANE'S FORD A FORDING PLACE OVER THE RAHWAY RIVER, USED BY GEN WASHINGTON IN HIS MANEUVERS, CRANFORD

EDISONS' SMALL VILLAGE PLANT LOCUST ST ROSELLE

GALLOPING HILL AND GALLOPING HILL RD. (ISSUE # 153)

SITE OF INDIAN VILLAGE TAMAQUES RESERVATION, WESTFIELD.

ABRAHAM CLARK HOUSE, CHESTNUT ST., ROSELLE.

MARSH HOUSE RAHWAY (ISSUE#54)

GIRL SCOUT HOUSE ONCE A FAMOUS INN AND STAGE STOP, ST. GEORGES AVE, RAHWAY (ISSUE # 24)

INDIAN MORTAR IN BAUMANNS YARD, ST. GEO. AVE. RAHWAY (ISSUE # 55)

UNION COUNTY

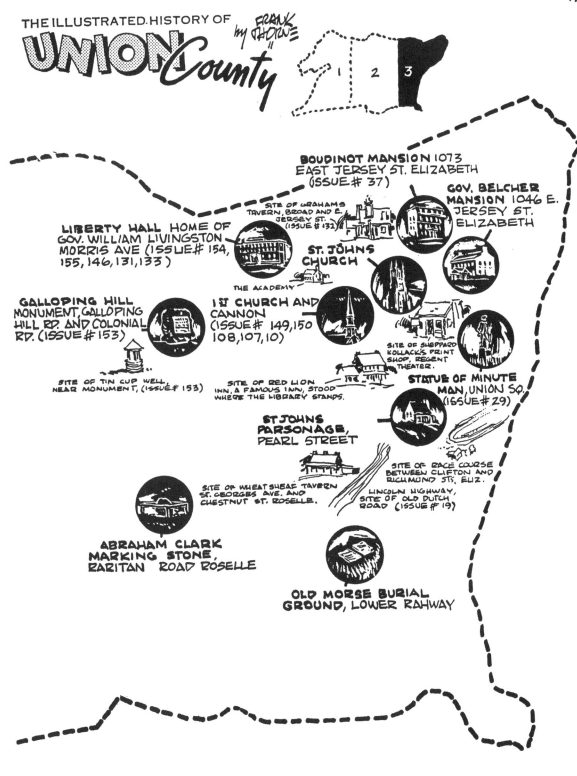

THE ILLUSTRATED HISTORY OF UNION County

by FRANK THORNE

> THE HISTORY OF OUR COUNTY IS BUT THE HISTORY OF GREAT MEN AND WOMEN.

LEFT TO RIGHT STAND: *HENRY HUDSON, PHILIP CARTERET, GOVERNOR WILLIAM LIVINGSTON, YOUNG ALEXANDER HAMILTON, SETTLER JOHN OGDEN, ELIAS BOUDINOT, ABRAHAM CLARK, THE UNKNOWN SOLDIER OF SPRINGFIELD, PARSON JAMES CALDWELL, OLD BALTUS ROLL, AUNT BETTY FRAZEE, AND MR. AND MRS. FRENCH.* AS YOU CAN SEE, WE RAN OUT OF ROOM! BUT IN OUR HEARTS ARE *GEORGE WASHINGTON, REVEREND JONATHAN DICKENSON*—THE LIST IS LONG—AND TENS OF THOUSANDS OF HARD-WORKING FARM FOLK, SLAVES, INDIANS...MOTHERS, FATHERS, DAUGHTERS...ALL PART OF THE TAPESTRY OF HISTORY THAT MADE UNION THE UNEQUALED COUNTY IN NEW JERSEY!

"OLD FIRST" FROM A NINETEENTH CENTURY PRINT.

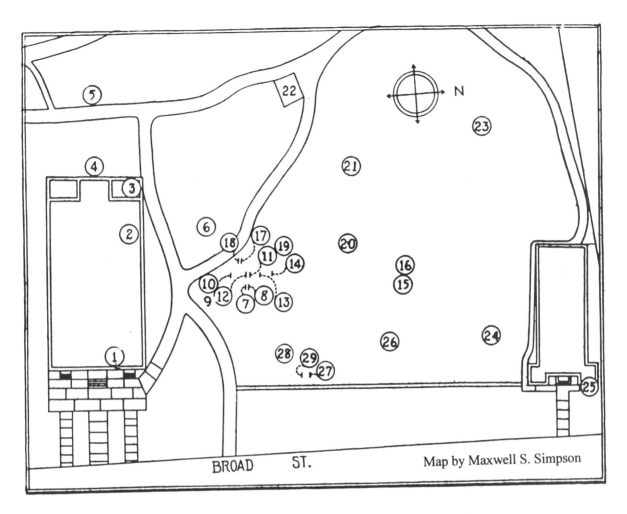

Map by Maxwell S. Simpson

EXTRAORDINARY DESTINATIONS...

MANY OF THE HEROES AND HEROINES OF THE COLONIAL PERIOD IN UNION COUNTY REST IN THE CEMETERY OF THE FIRST PRESBYTERIAN CHURCH ON BROAD STREET IN ELIZABETH IN THE SHADOW OF THE UNION COUNTY COURTHOUSE. A VISIT TO THIS HALLOWED GROUND WILL BE A MOVING EXPERIENCE, THE NUMBERED *MAP WILL GUIDE YOU.

1. S.A.R. BRONZE TABLET 2. PHINNEY STONE IN WALL 3. LAWRENCE BROTHERS CHOIR ROOM
4. PARSON CALDWELL AND WIFE 5. GEN. ELIAS DAYTON VAULT 6. JOSIAH HUNT, PATRIOT
7. JNO. OGDEN 8. BENJ. OGDEN 9. COL. AARON OGDEN 10. MARY OGDEN BARBER 11. GEN.
MATHIAS OGDEN 12. HANNAH OGDEN 13. STEPHEN CRANE, MAGISTRATE 14. GEN. WILLIAM
CRANE 15. CALDWELL MONUMENT 16. REV. JONATHAN DICKENSON 17. ANN BARBER, WIDOW
OF FRANCES BARBER 18. MOSES OGDEN 19. ELIAS BOUDINOT 20. REV. JOHN HARRIMAN,
FIRST PASTOR 1687 21. MICHAEL MEGIE 22. REV. NICHOLAS MURRAY MONUMENT
23. CORNELIUS HETFIELD 24. MRS. ROBERTSON (CALDWELL) WAS THE BABE IN ARMS WHEN
MRS. CALDWELL WAS MURDERED. 25. COLONIAL DAMES TABLET 26. REV JOHN MCDOWELL
MONUMENT 27. HANNAH ARNETT TABLET 28. CAPT. WILLIAM BRITTEN 29. SHEPARD KOLLACK

♦REPRODUCED FROM *HISTORIC ELIZABETH 1664-1914*, PUBLISHED BY THE ELIZABETH DAILY JOURNAL

THE DESERTED VILLAGE

HUDDLED NEAR THE HIGH WALLS THAT CONTAIN THE TRAFFIC'S ROAR ON ROUTE 78 IS WHAT REMAINS OF THE *DESERTED VILLAGE*. IT IS ONE OF THE MOST BEAUTIFUL SETTINGS IN UNION COUNTY. ON PAGE 117 WE READ THE STORY OF THE WILLCOXIE (LATER CHANGED TO WILLCOCKS) FAMILY AND PETER'S MILL. *YOU WILL FIND THAT PARTS OF THE MILL'S FOUNDATION ARE STILL VISIBLE!*

THE FAMILY CEMETERY RESTS ON THE HEIGHTS BEHIND THE CHURCH/STORE. MORE THAN A DOZEN SOULS SLEEP ON THAT RISE. THE INSCRIPTIONS ON THE GRAVESTONES ARE INTRIGUING: JOHN WILLCOCKS SR. OF THE N.J. LIGHT HORSE MILITIA, AND JOHN WILLCOCKS, PERHAPS HIS SON, BOTH DIED ON DECEMBER 22, 1776, AS DID PHEBE BADGLEY WILLCOCKS. *WHAT TRAGIC EVENT TOOK ALL THREE TO ETERNITY THAT FATEFUL DAY?*

DAVID FELT, ANOTHER ENTERPRISING MILLER TOOK POSSESSION OF THE LAND IN THE 19TH CENTURY AND BUILT A TOWERING WOODEN PAPER MILL NEAR THE OLD MILL. OVER A DOZEN COTTAGES WERE CONSTRUCTED TO HOUSE THE MILL-WORKERS. THE COMMUNITY BECAME KNOWN AS *FELTVILLE*. IT THRIVED FOR MANY YEARS UNTIL COMPETITION FROM BIGGER MORE MODERN MILLS MADE FELT'S OPERATION OBSOLETE. AFTER THE CIVIL WAR IT BECAME A HOLIDAY SPOT NAMED *GLENSIDE PARK* WHICH FEATURED A HOTEL AND RECREATIONAL FACILITIES. THE MASKER BARN HOUSED THE CARRIAGES THAT BROUGHT THE HOTEL GUESTS FROM FAR AND WIDE.

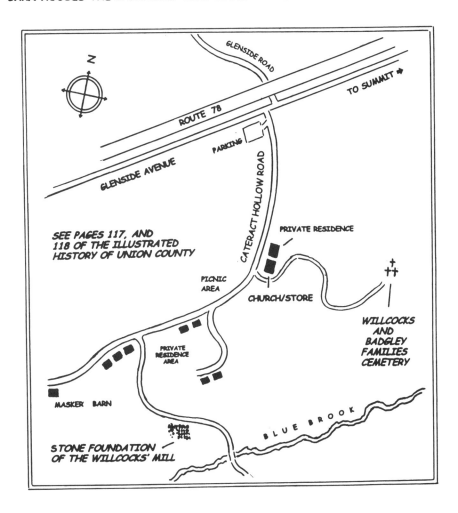

THE COPPER MINE

THE OLD MINE IS LOCATED UPSTREAM FROM THE DESERTED VILLAGE. WHILE YOU'RE IN THE AREA DRIVE OVER TO THE TRAILSIDE MUSEUM AND TAKE THE GREEN TRAIL TO THE ORANGE AND THEN THE PATH TO THE MINE. MANY YEARS AFTER THE DUTCH ABANDONED THE PROJECT THE SETTLERS WORKED THE MINE. TO THIS DAY TRACES OF COPPER ORE CAN STILL BE FOUND IN THE AREA!

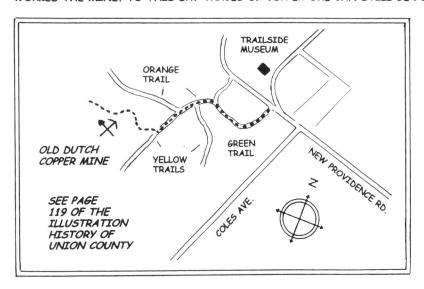

LIBERTY HALL MUSEUM AND THE MERCHANTS AND DROVERS TAVERN

A <u>MUST</u> DESTINATION IS THE *LIBERTY HALL MUSEUM 1003 MORRIS AVE. UNION*, IT IS AN ABSORBING CHRONICLE OF UNION COUNTY HISTORY OFFERING GUIDED TOURS AND A 10 MINUTE ORIENTATION FILM. OPEN 10AM TO 4PM WEDNESDAY THRU SUNDAY. SUNDAY HOURS—NOON UNTIL 3PM. CALL 908 527 0400

THE MERCHANTS AND DROVERS TAVERN STILL PROUDLY STANDS ON THE CORNER OF WESTFIELD AVE. AND ST. GEORGES AVE. IN RAHWAY. NOW COMPLETELY RESTORED, THE BUILDING IS OPEN FROM 10AM TO 4PM ON THURSDAYS AND FRIDAYS AND THE FIRST AND THIRD WEEKENDS FROM 1PM TO 4PM. CALL 732 381 0441

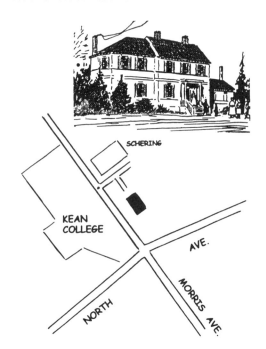

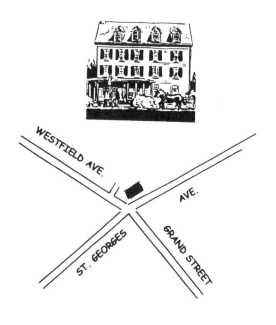

INDEX

The evacuated Elizabethtown patriots watch helplessly as Reverend Caldwell's home is torched by the retreating British forces.